FULL OF YEARS

FULL

OF

YEARS

Aging and the Elderly in the Bible and Today

STEPHEN SAPP

Abingdon Press
Nashville

Full of Years:
Aging and the Elderly in the Bible and Today

Copyright © 1987 by Abingdon Press

This book is printed on acid-free paper.

Library of Congress Cataloging-in-Publication Data

Sapp, Stephen.
Full of years.
Bibliography: p.
Includes index.
1. Aged in the Bible. 2. Bible—Criticism, interpretation,
etc. 3. Aged—Religious life. I. Title.

BS680.A34S26   1987   261.8'3426   87-1840
ISBN 0-687-13710-1
(alk. paper)

Quotations from *The Age of Triage: Fear and Hope in an Overcrowded World* reprinted
by permission of the author. Copyright © 1983 by Richard L. Rubenstein.

Quotations from "Who Cares for the Elderly?" by William F. May reproduced by
permission. Copyright © the Hastings Center.

"Morningside" by Neil Diamond copyright © 1972 Prophet Music, Inc. All rights
reserved. Used by permission.

Scripture quotations are from the Revised Standard Version of the Bible,
copyrighted 1946, 1952, © 1971, 1973 by the Division of Christian Education of
the National Council of the Churches of Christ in the U.S.A., and are used by
permission.

MANUFACTURED BY THE PARTHENON PRESS AT
NASHVILLE, TENNESSEE, UNITED STATES OF AMERICA

To
L. J. and Lottie Mae Brewer Sapp
and
Mary Adele Chave Manley

for love, support, and encouragement beyond measure or gratitude, and for practical demonstration of graceful aging.

CONTENTS

FOREWORD

In this volume Stephen Sapp has
dealt in a scholarly way with almost every imaginable aspect
of aging and the elderly. It is a must, in my opinion, for
anyone who would have a comprehensive knowledge of the
multiple aspects of individuals' growing old. The author
starts the volume with a recital of the significance of the
elderly in our population. For example, he points out that
when the federal census was first taken in 1790, those 65
and older comprised less than 2 percent of the total
population of the fledgling nation (accounting for one in
every fifty Americans). By 1900 the proportion had grown to
only 4 percent, or approximately 3 million persons, and
fewer than 20 percent of Americans lived from birth to age
70; today those 65 and older comprise approximately 12

percent of the population (accounting for one in every nine) and over 80 percent of those born will live to age 70. A reasonable expectation is that by the year 2030, 65 million Americans will be 65 or older, a number two and one-half times greater than that of the elderly population in 1980, and roughly 21 percent of the total projected population (and possibly more than the number of those under 25).

The author points out that Americans born in 1985 could expect to live to be 75, 27 years longer than someone born in 1900. In 1985, over 2 million people had their sixty-fifth birthday (5,600 a day), while 1.5 million who were 65 or older died. The net gain of more than 560,000 represents a daily increase of 1,540 elderly Americans.

Within 50 years it is expected that approximately 20 percent of the American population will be over 65. The fastest growing group of the elderly population is those over 85. The significance of these figures is that for the first time in human history, a society exists in which most of its members live to be old.

These factors have an important impact upon our society. Old age is no longer a rarity, and therefore, in the opinion of some, old age is not as much respected or regarded with as much awe as when it was more rare. Besides, our nation and those who plan for its future have to recognize the impact of our aging population upon our economy, upon the attitude of the government toward the elderly. We must give thought to the arrangements that the government must make for the sustenance, the medical assistance, and the other provisions necessary to enable them to live the kind of good life we feel they are entitled to live. We have by recent legislation assured the elderly that they cannot be mandatorily retired on account of age, thereby opening up to them the continued right to work if they are ready, willing, and able to do so, and to continue to have a major part in the life of the country to which their long lives have contributed so much. The author gives us the full picture of the new place that the elderly have in our nation's population and in our national life, and the various aspects of the blessings and the problems that an enlarging elderly population presents to the nation.

Two chapters of the volume present a thorough examination of Old and New Testament Scripture on aging and the obligations due to the elderly. The references Dr. Sapp discusses include not only the commandment "Honor thy father and mother" but also numerous other biblical statements on the elderly. The Bible contains many references to the inevitability of aging, and the usual weakening of the individual on account of the aging process, but aging is emphasized as a source of wisdom. The elderly are referred to with respect, indeed with reverence. Both the Old and New Testaments show the importance of the elderly in the community and emphasize that the younger should always be concerned with the needs of the elderly and strive to meet those needs. While the Scriptures emphasize the superiority of the spirit over the body, they nevertheless make clear the sacredness of the body as a creation of God. The Scriptures put special emphasis on the elderly widow and clearly recite the obligation of the younger, especially members of the family of the elderly, to attend the needs of, and to profoundly respect the dignity of, the elderly. These Scripture references afford the moral basis for our reverence and respect for the elderly and for the assistance we feel is due to those who are "old and full of years."

The final chapter in this volume concerns the obligation of other members of our society toward the elderly. Emphasized are the problems presented by the elderly, for example, their increasing numbers. There is conflict about the debt we owe to the elderly, as compared to the debt we owe the younger. Some see the elderly as too often obstructing promotion and the proper progress of those who are younger. It is pointed out by some that the elderly are already the subject of special care by our society, being the recipients of Social Security benefits and a certain amount of medical care through Medicare and Medicaid, as well as other plans also for the benefit of the elderly. These preferred benefits enjoyed by the elderly, in these people's opinions, diminish the obligation of children and other members of our society to give particular assistance to the elderly. The author makes it clear, however, that the elderly deserve all the benefits bestowed upon them, and in fact, many more, such as more comprehensive medical care, more and better housing, more access to good meals, more transportation facilities, more recreational opportunities, and the like. The author in a vivid way depicts how the elderly stand out as a special group of people who have travelled far along the road of life, who have done much for the country—more than any other group—and who are upon the last part of that long journey. They deserve special consideration, because if they don't get it now, it will not come in this life. That last part of the long journey should be as healthy and as long and as happy as it can be made by a grateful society and grateful families. The author in this volume has given the reader a thorough and comprehensive view of the elderly and their place in the Bible, in history, and in our society today. He has examined and clearly presented all aspects of the relationships of the elderly for readers who would understand the elderly in all their manifold relationships to the past and to the present. They should read, indeed study, this valuable volume.

Perhaps nothing sums up better the general meaning of this excellent book than the quotation the author gives us from the poet Browning:

Grow old along with me!
The best is yet to be,
The last of life, for which the first was made . . .

CLAUDE PEPPER
Eighteenth Congressional District
Florida

PREFACE

When I began my career in the academic study of religion, my area of research was the ethics of human sexuality. Some four years ago, I shifted my attention to aging and began the research that has culminated in this book. When I told a colleague about my new direction, he said that he was not surprised: He had already discovered that as one approaches forty, one's thoughts (and interests) naturally shift from sex to aging!

I do not think that was *my* reason. As this book makes clear, of the many pressing issues facing the United States, one of the most critical is the stunning increase in the number of elderly people expected to occur over the next half-century. Any attempt to deal with this unprecedented demographic phenomenon must be based on an understanding of the nature and purpose of human life, and thus discussion of the topic is ultimately a *religious* matter. I hope I have contributed to this vital discussion.

Many people have played a role in the writing of this

15

book, and though the danger exists of neglecting someone who merits recognition, several deserve special mention.

A mere expression of gratitude does not do justice to the contributions of the other members of the Department of Religious Studies at the University of Miami. Daniel Pals, my chairman, read every chapter and supported the entire enterprise in ways too numerous to mention. John Fitzgerald and Marvin Sweeney read various chapters dealing with their particular areas and made suggestions that greatly improved the final product. Above all, they have been friends and colleagues in every sense of the words.

Among others I want to thank are the following:

- The University of Miami Research Council, which granted me a Max Orovitz Summer Research Award in 1984 that supported the early research for this book;
- The members and staff of the Moorings Presbyterian Church in Naples, Florida, who taught me much about successful aging;
- The Honorable Claude Pepper, who not only took time from his busy schedule to read the manuscript and contribute a foreword but who also and more significantly personifies what I have tried to say in this book about both dealing with one's own aging and meeting one's responsibilities to the elderly;
- Harmon L. Smith, teacher and friend, who read the manuscript and made typically helpful suggestions, all of which I wish I had been able to incorporate;
- William M. Clements, who, in addition to reading the manuscript, has supported my work in this area from its inception;
- Michael Lawrence of Abingdon Press, whose central role in bringing this book to print is greatly appreciated, and Rebecca Marnhout, whose careful copyediting improved the readability of the manuscript considerably;

• My mother-in-law, Mary C. Manley, who graciously contributed her professional editorial expertise throughout the writing of the book;

• My parents, L. J. and Lottie B. Sapp, whose example, especially in their interactions with my grandmother, has taught me a great deal about Christian love and intergenerational relationships;

• My sons Eric and David, who shared their father with a word processor for over two years with patience, good humor, and encouragement unexpected in ones so young.

Finally, as always, my greatest debt is to Mary, who knows how much of this book is hers and how much better it is for her contributions. I cannot yet know if Robert Browning is correct that "the best is yet to be," but I know that I am greatly blessed to have Mary to "grow old along with me."

INTRODUCTION

Grow old along with me!
The best is yet to be,
The last of life, for which the first was made;
Our times are in His hand
Who saith, "A whole I planned,
Youth shows but half; trust God: see all, nor be afraid!"

So wrote Robert Browning in "Rabbi
ben Ezra"—and inspiring, uplifting words they are. The
poet's sentiment, of course, was nothing new, reflecting an
idea long expressed in the history of human thought.
Seneca, for example, wrote in the first century C.E., "Life is
most delightful when it is on the downward slope," a claim
preceded by several centuries in the Hebrew Bible's
affirmation, "A hoary head is a crown of glory" (Prov. 16:31).

So much for noble ideals and encouraging sentiments. The
reality of being old in America today is more accurately

expressed, not in Browning's sentimental idealism, but in the words of a contemporary poet (songwriter Neil Diamond):

> Morningside,
> The old man died
> And no one cried
> They simply turned away
> And when he died
> He left a table made of nails and pride
> And with his hands, he carved these words inside
> "For my children"
> . . . .
> Morningside
> An old man died
> And no one cried
> He surely died alone
> And truth is sad
> For not a child would claim the gift he had
> The words he carved became his epitaph
> "For my children"

Robert Butler is less poetic but more explicit when he says, "For many elderly Americans old age is a tragedy, a period of quiet despair, deprivation, desolation and muted rage"—and this in an ominously titled book, *Why Survive? Being Old in America.*[1] Congressman Claude Pepper, one of the most forceful advocates for the elderly today, demands an end to ageism—"as vicious, arbitrary and indefensible as racism and sexism"—and affirms that "it is time that older people received the same protection against arbitrary treatment as others whose civil rights have been systematically violated."[2] Martin Marty, who according to *Time* magazine is "generally acknowledged to be the most influential living interpreter of religion in the U.S.,"[3] provides a sad but true summary of the situation when he affirms, "In contemporary America, older people are almost always lumped together and classified as a *problem.*"[4] Given this gap between the ideal and the real, one must ask what, if anything, can be done to bring the American experience of aging and old age into accord with the experience of earlier generations cited above.

A society determines its treatment of the elderly based upon the significance it gives to old age, which in turn rests upon the society's understanding of the nature and the purpose of life itself. And an understanding of the nature and the purpose of life stems largely from the society's religious traditions, even if those traditions are not espoused formally by a sizable segment of the population (indeed, some would say that religion itself can be defined as that in which one finds the meaning of life, whether or not it is called "religion"). In order to comprehend the situation in which contemporary American society finds itself with regard to the vital question of aging and the elderly, then, and especially to begin to formulate solutions to the many problems this issue raises, one must be familiar with the predominant religious traditions that have shaped the beliefs, the practices, and the attitudes of the nation. These traditions have their foundation in the sacred scriptures of Judaism and Christianity.

Like all ethical reflection within scripturally based religious traditions, this book is dialogical: It seeks to bring the message of ancient texts into conversation with the concerns of a modern society. This task carries with it a dual obligation: to interpret the sacred and to address the secular. Thus, after a preliminary survey of the current situation of the elderly in this country and some of the ethical issues involved, two chapters of the book examine the sacred writings of Judaism and Christianity—the Hebrew Bible (or Old Testament, in Christian terminology) and the New Testament—to discover what they say about old age, the process of aging, and older people.

This interpretation of Scripture will provide the necessary foundation for the fourth and fifth chapters, which address the contemporary issues of aging in light of biblical perspectives. This method insures an approach to the subject of aging and the elderly that is informed by the foundational documents of Christianity, faithful to their message, and sensitive to the current situation.

This inquiry is complicated somewhat by the fact that the Bible does not address "aging" in exactly the categories that a modern interpreter might like, just as it does not consider directly many other topics that one might wish it did. In the Bible's more holistic approach to human existence, the departmentalization so familiar to contemporary Western society is simply lacking. Thus there occur few directives aimed at the elderly as such, and little explicit consideration of issues that are widely discussed today and about which one would like to have a definitive biblical word. As will become apparent, however, even if the Bible does not often speak directly *to* the elderly, it still has some significant things to say *about* aging, the aged, and their proper treatment.

Indeed, it is impossible to examine in detail all of the statements in the Bible that pertain to aging and the elderly. The Old Testament alone, for example, contains about 250 references to old age. This study will therefore of necessity be selective, treating in some depth only those passages and texts that give the greatest help and guidance to the basic quest—to discover what the source documents of the biblical tradition have to say concerning attitudes toward aging and responsibilities toward the elderly.

An important issue must be raised at the outset, namely, the question of the general relationship of the Bible and contemporary Christian ethics. A number of excellent books have appeared in recent years that address this significant hermeneutical issue, and they reward careful reading.[5] The Bible was written by people whose knowledge of the workings of the world differed greatly from the findings of modern scientific inquiry, and attitudes toward the Bible, its interpretation, and its authority have varied widely throughout Christian history. Nevertheless, Christians have always found the Bible to be a collection of documents that communicate timely and compelling truths even in the vastly changed situations in which believers have found themselves, and this ancient book has managed to retain a central and definitive place in Christianity.

As always, the danger exists that one will approach the Bible, not with the goal of discovering what it says to the reader on a particular issue, but rather in the hope of finding from it support for what one already believes. Aware of this danger—and conscious of the illegitimacy of proof-texting, however sophisticated it might be made to appear—the Christian interpreter nonetheless must take very seriously the witness of the Old and the New Testaments in making any statement on a contemporary issue. As Bruce Birch and Larry Rasmussen put it, "Christian ethics is not Christian ethics unless the Bible is normative in some important way for the Christian life."[6]

As should be apparent, this work is ultimately neither a methodological study nor an exegetical monograph; it is rather an exercise in constructive ethical reflection, which takes as a basic starting point that Scripture still speaks to Christians on issues crucial to living a Christian life. The primary goal is to suggest an appropriate Christian response to the dilemma of dealing with the rapidly increasing number (and percentage) of elderly persons in the population, in the face of marriage, family, and work patterns that are undergoing significant changes. As a *Christian* ethicist I have tried to take seriously, and to be responsible to, the biblical material, in the belief that any legitimate Christian statement on a topic of contemporary concern must be firmly grounded in the Bible. I do not pretend to have finally answered all technical questions of methodology or exegesis—or, in many cases, even to have raised them.

One further preliminary question needs consideration: What is aging? Who are the elderly? Obviously, what constitutes "old" age—that is, the point at which one becomes "old"—has changed over the centuries. What was "old" at various periods in biblical times may not be so today. For example, the Old Testament records the ages at death of fourteen kings of the Davidic dynasty (who ruled between 926 and 597 B.C.E.), and the average is only forty-four. Given that royal heirs received special care and attention when young and that adult kings certainly had many advantages over the common people, life expectancy across the society must have been even lower.[7] Indeed, one of the most far-ranging debates in rabbinic interpretation of Torah concerns precisely who does and does not qualify for the honor commanded to be shown to an "elder" or "old man" (Lev. 19:32*b*).[8]

Selection of an arbitrary chronological age to designate someone as old, therefore, is very difficult, especially when one is dealing with societies far removed in time and place. The United States has chosen sixty-five or seventy as the generally accepted age at which one is considered to be old (at least in terms of maximum economic productivity);[9] everyone knows people well in excess of that age, however, who are "old" by designation only, and others considerably younger who exhibit clear signs of aging. In this book, then, *aging* will refer to normal biological processes that lead to a decline in physical/mental powers in the later stages of a person's life, with attendant social, cultural, psychological, and other ramifications. The *aged* or *elderly* will be those who have at least begun to experience this multifaceted decline. This approach seems to be in line with the actual practice of the cultures that will be examined (with certain notable exceptions) and thus has the advantage of letting the sources dictate their own subject matter.

Furthermore, a little reflection on the topic reveals two

24

inextricably interrelated but nonetheless distinguishable issues:

1. one's understanding of and attitude toward aging itself (particularly one's own); and
2. one's sense of obligation toward the aged, which determines one's willingness to interact with, learn from, give value to, and assist them—including one's own parents!—through this stage of their lives.

Although it seems intuitively obvious that (2) is largely dependent upon (1), such a relationship is apparently not so clearly recognized in the everyday lives of most Americans—witness all the problems associated with aging and the treatment of the elderly in this society![10] Throughout the book, this twofold approach will inform the examination of the relevant materials and will guide reflection upon them.

In an essay entitled "Education for Ministry with the Aging," Melvin A. Kimble suggests that "aging is a multidimensional reality that demands an interdisciplinary approach." He next offers the important reminder that "any examination of aging and the aged should reflect an understanding that it is a *whole person* who is aging and is aged." Kimble then suggests that the "insights of medicine, sociology, psychology, and theology need to be brought into dynamic dialogue if an integrated understanding of the older adult is to emerge."[11] This book is an effort to contribute from the last of these necessary perspectives. As such, it will speak both to those who simply want to know what the basic source documents of two of the world's major religions have to say about this topic, and to those who themselves stand consciously within one of those religions, consider its teachings in some way normative for their behavior, and are struggling to find in their faith tradition some help and guidance on this vital topic.

25

NOTES

1. Robert Butler, *Why Survive? Being Old in America* (New York: Harper & Row, 1975), p. 2.

2. Claude Pepper, *Ask Claude Pepper* (Garden City, N.Y.: Doubleday, 1984), p. 28.

3. Richard N. Ostling, "Telling America What It Believes," *Time* (December 22, 1986): 59.

4. Martin Marty, "Cultural Antecedents to Contemporary American Attitudes toward Aging," in William M. Clements, ed., *Ministry with the Aging: Designs, Challenges, Foundations* (New York: Harper & Row, 1981), p. 56.

5. Two helpful books among many on this topic are Bruce C. Birch and Larry L. Rasmussen, *Bible and Ethics in the Christian Life* (Minneapolis: Augsburg Publishing House, 1976); and Thomas W. Ogletree, *The Use of the Bible in Christian Ethics: A Constructive Essay* (Philadelphia: Fortress Press, 1983). For a useful recent review of the ongoing methodological debate (albeit dealing with a different subject), see Lisa Sowle Cahill, *Between the Sexes: Foundations for a Christian Ethics of Sexuality* (Philadelphia: Fortress Press; New York: Paulist Press, 1985), especially chapter 2.

6. Birch and Rasmussen, *Bible and Ethics*, p. 47.

7. Hans Walter Wolff, *Anthropology of the Old Testament*, trans. Margaret Kohl (Philadelphia: Fortress Press, 1974), p. 119.

8. For a brief review of this controversy, see Norman Lamm, ed., *The Good Society: Jewish Ethics in Action* (New York: Viking Press, 1974), pp. 119-31.

9. The story of the selection of sixty-five as the age of "senescence" in the United States is a remarkable one. According to David P. Barash (*Aging: An Exploration* [Seattle: University of Washington Press, 1983], pp. 207-8) the Social Security Administration chose sixty-five as the age for the reception of benefits because Bismarck had set that age in Germany in 1881 for the first modern old-age pension system. Bismarck, fearful of a Marxist revolution, considered a government pension good insurance against civil unrest. His actuaries assured him that few nineteenth-century Germans lived past sixty-five, and the choice of that age for the reception of benefits thus served Bismarck's political purposes without risking an undue drain on the treasury. On the basis of the German standard, over fifty years later the United States selected the age of sixty-five for its "pension" system. Barash concludes, "If Bismarck's criteria were to be employed today, the age at retirement would probably be ninety or more."

10. For example, John Deedy, in a helpful book on intergenerational relationships (*Your Aging Parents* [Chicago: Thomas More Press, 1984], pp. 23, 26), makes the point clear: "Aging does things to people, which is why an understanding of one's own aging is vital to the process of understanding one's aged parents [or, one may add, *any* older person]. . . . Aging is the one inescapable fact in all our lives, and . . . those of us who are blind to the fact of our own aging will never understand the aging problems of our aged parents."

11. Melvin A. Kimble, "Education for Ministry with the Aging," in Clements, *Ministry with the Aging*, p. 211.

CONTEMPORARY ISSUES: SETTING THE STAGE

CHAPTER ONE

The issues of age in the 80s chal-
lenge every discipline, every institution, especially religious
institutions, every nation-state, every human group, and
every creature."[1] So writes Maggie Kuhn, one of the most
effective voices for the elderly in America today. The
challenge might be less disturbing were not so many other
authorities expressing doubts about the resources and
guidelines available to meet it. Consider two highly
regarded researchers in the field, Joseph A. Kuypers and
Vern L. Bengston, writing about the "profoundly conflic-
tual loyalties" felt by members of older families: "Culture
provides inadequate or inaccurate normative guidance.
Social supports are underdeveloped or hard to access, and
the whole family is left vulnerable to moralisms concerning
'duty' or 'loyalty.' "[2] And Stephen Z. Cohen and Bruce
Michael Gans contend that "the traditional definition of an
adult's responsibilities toward an aging parent are now
largely outmoded or inadequate."[3]

Such allegations do not fall lightly upon the ears of those who stand in the biblical tradition, and these claims demand serious consideration by Christians. Before this can be done, however, it is necessary to have an understanding of the major factors that have brought about the situation that is the subject of such concern.

Some Statistics

The significant demographic changes occurring in this country are well known by now, and some of the problems they raise have received wide exposure as well. Furthermore, the ethical questions that Christians must address are not dependent upon the number of elderly persons or upon how rapidly they are increasing in proportion to the rest of the population. If the number of older people were decreasing, yet *any* were being treated inhumanely, a Christian would have to raise serious questions. Still, a few numbers will help to set the stage and to point up the magnitude of the problems that contemporary American society faces as it moves into the twenty-first century.[4]

When the first federal census was taken in 1790, those 65 and older comprised less than 2 percent of the total population of the fledgling nation (only one in every fifty Americans); by 1900 the proportion had grown to only 4 percent, or approximately 3 million persons; today the comparable figures are approximately 12 percent 65 and over (about one in every nine, or approaching 30 million). In 1900, fewer than 20 percent of Americans could expect to live from birth to age 70; today over 80 percent can expect to reach that age. The number of older people in the population is expected to continue to grow; in fact, those over 55 are the *only* age group likely to show significant growth during the next century. The growth rate will taper off during the next decade because of the relatively small number of births during the years of the Depression and

World War II,[5] but between 2010 and 2030, when the "baby boom" cohort reaches 65, a rapid increase will occur. Projections are risky and vary according to assumed fertility and immigration rates; still, a reasonable expectation is that by the year 2030, 65 million Americans will be 65 or older, a number two and one-half times greater than the elderly population in 1980 and roughly 21 percent of the total projected population (and possibly more than the number of those under 25).

Furthermore, the older segment of the population is itself becoming older, which has major implications for their care, as will become apparent later. Between 1900 and 1985, those aged 65–74 increased in number almost eight times, but those 75–84 increased eleven times, and those 85 and older twenty-two times. Even more strikingly, since 1980, the last group—termed by demographers the "oldest old"—has grown 19 percent (to 2.7 million) while those 75–84 have increased 12 percent (to 8.8 million) and those 65–74, 7 percent (to 17 million).

As for life expectancy, an American born in 1985 could expect to live to be almost 75, 27 years more than someone born in 1900. Though the major reason for this increase is reduced death rates for children and young adults, life expectancy at 65 has increased by 2.5 years since 1960 (after increasing by only 2.4 years from 1900 to 1960). In fact, a person reaching 65 in 1985 could expect to live another 16.8 years (14.6 for males and 18.6 for females). By 1990, one of every four people reaching 65 is expected to live at least another 20 years.

Finally, in 1985 about 2.1 million people marked their sixty-fifth birthday (5,600 a day), while 1.5 million who were 65 and older died. The net gain of more than 560,000 represents a *daily* increase of 1,540 elderly Americans.[6]

An interesting conjecture may be made here concerning the mere fact of the increase in numbers of elderly people in

29

society today. Although human values almost certainly do not operate according to the laws of classical economics, a parallel exists between the increase in the *number* of elderly persons and the decrease in the *value* ascribed to them in contemporary American society. William F. May makes the point in language especially relevant to this study: "For the first time in history, becoming old is commonplace. This fact, as much as any other, may account for the special ways in which we break the fourth [*sic*] commandment today. Honor comes harder when the elderly are no longer rare."[7] In a similar vein, Robert Butler notes the paradox that the extension of life expectancy actually has lowered the social status of the elderly: "Longevity is no longer viewed with awe and envy now that it has been mass-produced through medical science."[8] When few old people existed, by virtue of that fact alone they took on value (which was doubtless augmented by other characteristics for which the aged traditionally have been respected, such as wisdom and experience); today, being quite common, the elderly seem less valuable. Perhaps some modified form of "supply and demand" is indeed at work here.

Some Problems and Issues

The demographic picture of this country for the next half-century, then, is fairly clear. Both the number and (probably of even greater significance) the proportion of the elderly in the overall population will continue to grow, most rapidly among the "oldest old." At the same time that these population shifts occur, a number of other major changes will continue to affect the way Americans live. Some of these changes have particular impact upon the situation of the elderly. Although no causal relationships can be proven between these trends and the demographic shifts, the fact that they all are occurring at the same time suggests (1) that mutual influences are at work that cannot be ignored, and (2) that some of the trends and shifts may assume heightened significance because of the concurrent existence of others. What are some of these changes in the American way of life that interact significantly with the "graying of America"?

Technological Advances

INCREASED LIFE EXPECTANCY   The first such change that demands mention is one that in a very real sense underlies this whole book and makes it necessary, namely, an amazing increase in life expectancy made possible by various technological advances, especially in the area of public health and medicine. As health care improvements have lowered mortality rates, the fertility rate has also decreased significantly (attributable at least in part to improved contraceptive technology), a situation leading to the demographic picture outlined above. Despite the claims of some "prolongevity" advocates,[9] the remarkable gains in life expectancy of the recent past are not likely to be matched in the future. Thus the age structure of the United States will depend almost completely on fertility rates.

The implications of this situation are clear. Lower mortality and longer life expectancy mean, quite simply, that for the first time in human history a society exists in which most of its members live to be old. More is involved than just that, however. The United States faces a momentous cultural shift now that the lives of large numbers of people extend far beyond the period of their work and child-rearing duties and obligations. Unfortunately, as will become apparent later, while medicine and public health have made great strides in lengthening life, no such attention has been given to improving the quality of the added years.

Although not strictly a "technological" change itself, this new situation is largely attributable to technology. Only one hundred years ago, three-quarters of American males 65 or

31

over were gainfully employed; today only about one-quarter are.[10] In earlier times, "retirement" in the modern sense of the word was rare; people worked until they simply could work no more. Today retirement is the norm, usually with little choice and at ever earlier ages, with a profound and often devastating impact upon those who retire. Furthermore, although the number of women in the work force has traditionally been small, women have experienced their own "maternal retirement" as a result of the demographic changes discussed above. Into the nineteenth century, American women had primarily maternal duties for their entire life spans, often rearing children right up to their own deaths. In 1850, for example, the mean age at death (61) was only two years greater than the age at which the mother's youngest child married; in 1950, the average mother was only 48 when her last child married, and she could expect over thirty more years of life. Women had been prepared for little else but mothering, and this role ended more suddenly, earlier in life, and with less societal recognition than did their husbands' careers. Many women thus found themselves even more affected by the "empty nest syndrome" than their husbands were by retirement.

These new conditions—a greatly increased number of arrivals into old age, and a considerable time to live after traditional "adult" duties are fulfilled—result largely from the rapid technological strides of the past century. That they have had and continue to have a significant impact on attitudes toward one's own aging and on both society's and individuals' understanding of their obligations toward the elderly is undeniable. A good illustration of this point lies in the fact that because of modern medical technology, death and aging (especially old age) have become closely linked. Until very recent times, death was not particularly associated with old age. In fact, the opposite was true: Throughout most of human history, death has been seen as the partner not of age but of infancy and childhood. To live to a ripe old age therefore meant that one had *avoided* death and was therefore a "death-defier." When so many people died in infancy or childhood—and even those who survived could expect to live but four or five decades—to reach "threescore and ten, or even by reason of strength fourscore" (Ps. 90:10), was indeed to cheat death and to acquire an aura of life rather than of death.

Today, however, the situation is reversed. In America, few die young. (Of course, *some* still do, but the fact that early death is *not* the expectation anymore is well illustrated by the shock, the extreme grief, the rage, and the sense of injustice that accompanies the death of a child, who "had his or her whole life ahead.") The longer one lives, therefore—once one reaches the stage that society considers "old"—the more one becomes a reminder to others not of life, but rather of "the last enemy."

The results of this situation are numerous, and none of them bodes well for the elderly person trying to make his or her way in contemporary society. An obvious outcome of the situation just described is that one comes to fear old age as indeed the final stage, the "waiting area" for death. Again, when death was associated with youth rather than with age, one could rejoice in having avoided premature death and having lived to be "an old man and full of years" (Gen. 25:8). When old age and death are seen as going hand in hand, however, one should not be surprised that most people do not look forward with relish to growing old.

Another result is that younger people do not like to have old people around because the elderly force one to confront one's own mortality. This is a problem that goes far deeper than any particular unpleasant characteristics or maladies that an older person may exhibit. Later, it will be argued that a significant factor in today's problems with aging is the widely held view that one's value depends not upon who one

33

is but upon what one does. Ironically, here is the other, but still negative, side of the point: In this case, it is simply the *fact* of being old, and thus serving as a reminder to others of their own transitory state of existence, that renders one distasteful, not anything that one does or does not do.

A related concern is the impact of the association of old age with death upon the elderly's sense of self-worth (which is essential to healthy functioning as a human being). When death comes to be seen as the natural, expected, and—increasingly—preferable outcome of aging, the death of an older person is not greeted with any great sense of loss. In fact, studies have shown that the least disturbing kind of death for a family and a community is that of an aged person. The death of an elderly parent has so little effect on many adult children that often no service or ceremony of any kind is held to acknowledge the death.

Apart from the impact that this situation may have on the children's opportunity to resolve their (obviously often unacknowledged) grief, the lack of notice given to the death of aged people can have a significant effect on two other groups. First, as already mentioned, when one observes the deaths of one's peers pass virtually unmarked, the logical conclusion to draw is that one's own death (surely the ultimate act of one's life and thus the final chance to "make a mark" upon the world) will cause hardly a ripple in the lives of those around one. Such a perception unavoidably contributes to a sense of diminished self-worth. A second group that may be adversely affected by the lack of importance attached to the death of the elderly is the third or fourth generation of the family (i.e., the grandchildren or great-grandchildren). At a time when their attitudes toward aging and the elderly are forming, to observe virtually no concern on the part of their parents or grandparents upon the death of an older relative might well indicate to them that the elderly (including their own parents) have no value and thus that they too will be of no significance when they grow old.

SHIFT TO AN INFORMATION SOCIETY Another significant change in contemporary culture that impinges directly upon the elderly arises from the "Information Revolution," that is, the shift from an industrial to an information society. The post-industrial society was originally thought to be based on services, but it has become increasingly clear that most of the "services" actually involve the creation, processing, and distribution of information. Whereas in an industrial society capital is the key, in the new society knowledge is the strategic resource. In such an economy, value rests not upon the kind of labor Marx analyzed but upon knowledge—most often, recently created and quickly outdated knowledge. Furthermore, as David Fischer points out, the "epistemic texture" of human knowledge has changed, away from knowledge gained from experience and tradition to knowledge based upon logic and formal proofs of reason. Whereas memory, vocabulary, and judgment tend to be more highly developed later in life, young adulthood is the peak period for achievement in mathematics, logic, and abstract reasoning.[11]

John Naisbitt suggests that the shift from an industrial to an information society is having as significant an impact as did the shift from an agricultural to an industrial society. In fact, the effects may be even greater because this revolution has occurred so quickly—in a mere twenty years compared to the century required by the shift from farm to factory.[12] One example of the impact of this "megashift" appears in Alvin Toffler's suggestion that "just as the nuclear family was promoted by the rise of the factory and office work, any shift *away* from the factory and office would also exert a heavy influence on the family."[13] Some evidence of this change—with significant implications for the elderly—is

35

already apparent, as the next section of this chapter will demonstrate.

Of great importance also to the concerns of this study are Naisbitt's provocative thoughts on the role of time in the megashift from an industrial to an information society:

> In our agricultural period, the time orientation was to the past. . . . The time orientation in an industrial society is *now*. . . . In our new information society, the time orientation is to the future. . . . We must now learn from the present how to anticipate the future. . . . we will be able to learn from the future the way we have been learning from the past.[14]

Such a change clearly has profound implications for attitudes toward aging and the elderly. Leo W. Simmons affirms in a landmark study that "perhaps the most striking fact about respect for old age is its widespread occurrence [in primitive societies]. Some degree of prestige for the aged seems to have been practically universal in all known societies."[15] Certainly among various reasons for this respect was the essential role played by the elderly as repositories of wisdom and the accumulated knowledge of the society. Not only did the elders tend to be the ones who possessed and transmitted sacred knowledge; they were also the source of vital practical information about how and when to plant, for example, or where and how to hunt.

An information society, however, values *tomorrow's* knowledge, not yesterday's, and such a society stores and transmits its data on floppy disks, not in old people's minds and stories. The elderly today thus have no clearly defined role to give them prestige, and certainly not an essential one. On the contrary, they are likely to be seen as anachronisms in a society that values only the future, and as a nonproductive drain upon that society's limited resources.[16] It is but a short step to considering the elderly marginal and therefore expendable members of society, especially if money is limited and other priorities (such as arms) appear unquestionable.

Support for this view comes from a convincing analysis by Irving Rosow of the treatment of the elderly in contemporary American society.[17] According to Rosow, the elderly suffer from both role and status attrition, with five concomitants. First, "the loss of roles excludes the aged from significant social participation and devalues them." Regardless of ability, the elderly are removed from the economic mainstream, within which most men (and increasingly many women) obtain their major self-identity and thus sense of self-worth. As a result the old become marginal and alienated from the larger society. They "tend to be tolerated, patronized, ignored, rejected, or viewed as a liability." Next, "old age is the first stage of life with systematic status loss for an entire cohort." Every phase before old age is marked with social growth and "advancement." With old age, people who shortly before were highly valued for performance and achievement suddenly are "redefined as old and obsolete," without having done anything to deserve such a judgment except survive. Furthermore, they have no way to change this judgment by their actions because their actions did not cause it. One of the heaviest blows of aging, in fact, may be coping with this marginalization and loss of esteem when there has been no personal failure, a situation for which nothing in one's life up to that point has prepared one.

This suggests a third element, the fact that "persons in our society are not socialized to the fate of aging." In earlier stages of life, one is prepared at least informally for each subsequent stage, and the roles and the expectations to come are defined. The expectations of old age, however, are not so defined, and because it is a largely "roleless" stage, one can hardly prepare for it. This competitive society does not prepare people for defeat and consequent loss of status, of which old age is an irreversible example. Fourth, "because society does not specify an aged role, the lives of the elderly are socially unstructured." Now members of the class "old," they have nothing to do for that reason alone. Because social duties in earlier stages of life generally structure one's existence, few older people are prepared for the almost total removal of such expectations and norms. The very "uselessness" of so many of the "retirement" activities urged upon the elderly to "keep them busy"—endless golf, bridge, arts and crafts, television, even travel—underlines the lack of any *socially* useful role for the elderly and clearly expresses society's judgment of what they are now "good for." The result is a sense of being at a loss as to what to do with all one's time, with one's *self* in a literal sense, often accompanied by anxiety and acute boredom. As a result, finally, "role loss deprives people of their social identity." If the self is in large part defined by one's social roles, the loss of those roles obviously is tantamount to loss of self and ego destruction.

Significant to this process is the fact that the individual does nothing to cause it and therefore is literally powerless to prevent it. Yet it will affect every person in this society who survives to old age. Clearly, one can take a twofold approach to the problem: First, one can try early on to come to grips with one's own aging in order to gain some of the preparation that, as noted above, society does not offer and also to defend one's ego against the onslaught of social role and status attrition; and second, one can do whatever is within one's power, on both an individual and a societal basis, to prevent such losses from happening. These matters will be the concern of the final two chapters of this book.

Changing Nature of the American Family

Several more societal factors with significant impact on the elderly may be considered together under the general heading of changes in the nature of the American family, most of which are well known and need little explication here. Because these changes challenge the traditional centrality of the family in caring for its elderly members, an understanding of what has been happening recently to the family is essential.

INCREASED NUMBER OF WOMEN IN THE WORK FORCE   A particularly problematic social change affecting the elderly, and one that is implicated in the others to be considered in this section, concerns the greatly increased number of women working outside the home today. Numerous studies have shown that the primary caregivers for the impaired elderly are the spouses of the invalids. Given that women in our society live longer and tend to marry older men, the caregiver in an elderly couple is thus usually the wife. The next major source of care, however, is children, whether in the same household or not.

Thus the problem arises. Traditionally in this country, women—the wife or, when she is dead or herself in need of care, most often a daughter or daughter-in-law—have been the primary family caregivers for the elderly. If an aged parent needed care, the assmption was that a daughter or daughter-in-law, who was "just a housewife anyway," would merely add that person's care to her child-rearing duties (or replace departing children with an arriving infirm parent). Indeed, Elaine Brody's research led her to comment that the "family support system" so dear to the hearts of social gerontologists is really only a euphemism for "adult daughters (and daughters-in-law), who are the true alternatives" to institutional care.[18]

Today, however, a majority of these women who once would have been available to care for an elderly parent are employed outside the home: Fewer than one in five American families now fits the description of a "traditional

39

family," that is, father at work and mother at home caring for children. In the last twenty years the number of married women with children at home who work outside the home has risen from 31 percent to 57 percent (some sources place the number as high as 65 percent). In 1984 women constituted 43 percent of the total paid work force. The trend is not the result only of necessity: In a 1985 Roper Organization national poll, 51 percent of the women surveyed responded that they would choose a paying job if they had to choose between a family and a career; in 1975, only 35 percent chose a job over family.[19]

Those who have traditionally been expected to provide care for elderly parents and who have been available to do so now must either assume an extremely stressful if not impossible dual obligation or simply decline the role of caregiver. Either way the situation and the psyche of the elderly person are keenly affected, as are those of the younger generation who face the choice. Once again a change in contemporary American society is having a profound impact on the elderly and raises serious questions about providing care for them.

SHRINKING FAMILIAL SUPPORT BASE Three more interrelated changes contribute to a shrinking familial support base for the care of elderly family members: later marriage, later childbearing, and fewer children.[20]

According to a U.S. Census Bureau study, in March 1985 the median age at marriage for women was 23.3 years and for men 25.5 years. These figures represent an increase of over two years since 1970 and the highest median age at marriage ever for women; the age for men is approaching the record set around the turn of the century.[21]

The trend toward later marriage has contributed to another important change in the family, namely, a later age for childbearing. Not long ago, a woman who had not had a child by the age of 35 could forget about becoming a mother; today, women five or even ten years older give serious consideration to having their first child. As a result, the mean age of new mothers has increased dramatically: From 1975 to 1978, for example, the number of women 30–34 having their first child rose 37 percent, and the number of those 35–39, 22 percent. In addition, data indicate that the periods that elapse between marriage and first childbirth and between children are greater than in the past.

Significantly, older parents who have delayed childbearing are much less likely than younger parents to depend on grandparents for child care (24 percent when mother's age is under 25 versus 14 percent when mother is over 30). As parents wait longer to have children, who themselves may well follow the same pattern, grandparents become increasingly older at the birth of their grandchildren. Despite increased life expectancy, therefore, interaction between the old and the young actually may decline. Furthermore, the likelihood of the middle generation's being caught between parents' nursing home costs and children's college (or even pre-school!) costs greatly increases with delayed childbearing.

The third element in the trio of causes of a shrinking familial support base is the trend toward fewer children. In 1973 women between 15 and 44 who had ever been married averaged 2.2 children; in 1982 the average was 1.9. This 15 percent decline was caused by a decrease from 19 to 11 percent in the proportion of women with four or more children while the number with two increased from 26 to 32 percent (women with one, three, or no children showed little change). In 1982, then, married women still became mothers at about the same rate as in 1973, but they tended to stop after having two children.[22]

What, then, is the upshot of this troika of changes in recent marriage and fertility patterns? As mentioned above, the most significant effect is a shrinking of the familial support base available to care for family members when they get old. Current demographic data indicate that this is precisely what is happening. For example, there were 21 people 80 and over for every 100 aged 60–64 in 1920; in 1979 the ratio of 53 to 100 meant that the chances that a person between 60 and 64 had a parent or other elderly relative still alive had considerably more than doubled. According to current projections, for every 100 people in the first half of their seventh decade in the year 2030, approximately 80 will still be alive in their ninth decade! As Shirley H. Rhine concludes, two important implications arise from these data: First, fewer children than in the past will be available to bear the cost (financial and otherwise) of caring for an elderly parent or parents; and second, the cost of such support will increase because of the tendency for parents and adult children to live apart.[23]

Nonetheless, virtually all observers of the situation of the elderly agree with Ethel Shanas that despite the general devaluation of the elderly in this country and their loss of status and roles, one area remains "in which old people do have a role and a safe haven. That safe harbor is within the family."[24] Indeed, the family is about the only realistic alternative to living alone or in an institution. If the family gets smaller, however, and the "younger" generations are increasingly older, fewer people will be available to care for the older old, and those who are will themselves be older and more likely to need care.

In fact, the increasing number of "elderly caring for elderly" warrants a brief comment. As more people live longer (into their eighth, ninth, even tenth decades), often those who are their primary caregivers are themselves old and subject to the same needs, stresses, and problems as the even older persons for whom they are responsible. According to a major study by the National Center for

Health Services Research, 2.2 million people provided care in 1982 to 1.2 million disabled persons 65 or older. The average age of the caregivers was 57, and one-third were 65 or over. Over half of those receiving care were 75 or older, creating many situations in which the "young old" provide care to the "old old."[25] Thus the question of who cares for older caregivers when the caregivers need care demands attention.

The effects of the changes being discussed can be seen by an examination of several aspects of the current situation of the elderly. Obviously one cannot live with one's children in old age if one has no children, but does the *number* of children one had make any difference? Census data show that the larger the number of children, the more likely an elderly parent is to live with one of the children. In fact, widows over 65 with only one child are only half as likely to live in families as those with the most children, and the chance of being institutionalized is over twice as great for those with the smallest families as for those with the largest families. Finally, the probability of family financial help to needy elderly can also be predicted by the number of children: Logically, the fewer children one has the lower the probability that help will be available.[26] Thus the shrinking familial support base means a reduced probability of financial help for the elderly and a heightened likelihood of their living alone or being institutionalized.

Of course, the immediately preceding discussion seems to assume that elderly parents *want* to live with their children. Shanas, after carefully reviewing recent research, offers the following conclusions: Two-thirds of all unmarried older persons, male and female, live alone, a figure representing one of every seven older men and one of every three older women (because women outlive men, more elderly men have living wives than vice versa, about two-thirds of men to one-third of women). Of all older married people, with children or without, only 12 percent share a home with one or

43

more of their children; for the unmarried elderly—single, widowed, or divorced—17 percent live in such a household.

These living arrangements generally reflect expressed preferences: Older people and their adult children both value independence. In fact, fewer than half as many people over 60 approve of sharing a home as do those 21–29, and the percent of approval decreases consistently with each added decade of age. In 1979 only one in three of those over 21 surveyed said sharing a home with an elderly parent was a "good idea." Older parents prefer to live close enough to their children to see them and particularly their grandchildren, but they want to have their own home as long as possible. The younger generation emphasizes the need for privacy, independence, and freedom to come and go as they wish.[27] The implications of these findings will be important for the concerns of the last two chapters of this book.

INCREASED INCIDENCE OF DIVORCE   Another change in the family with several ramifications for aging is the widely noted increase in divorce. Although efforts are being made to remedy the deficiency, little research has been carried out on the specific effects of divorce upon the elderly, and several researchers consider divorce one of the most neglected areas in gerontology. The lack of interest is perhaps attributable to the relatively low incidence of divorce among older persons, though longer life may provide increasing opportunity for the elderly to terminate unsuccessful marriages. At any rate, the increased divorce rate across the society at all ages means that more people will enter old age divorced. According to Bureau of the Census figures, about twice as many older people in the 1980s are divorced as was the case in the 1960s.[28] Furthermore, divorce among the elderly's children and grandchildren can deeply affect the older person.

As far as their own divorces are concerned, in addition to

all the difficulties attendant upon divorce for any person, the elderly—because of the dynamics of the aging process itself—may be especially vulnerable to feelings of loss, inadequacy, and failure, especially if the divorce is not wanted. Their chances of remarriage are certainly lower than for younger people (particularly so for elderly women, who in 1983 outnumbered elderly men by 149 to 100). The elderly divorced, again women in particular, are more likely than their married or widowed counterparts to have financial problems and appear to be less integrated into kinship support systems.[29]

This last observation suggests one of the most difficult aspects of the problem of divorce and the elderly, namely, that of increasingly complex intergenerational family relationships. In the first place, newly divorced elderly people may discover unexpected divisions of loyalty among their adult children and even grandchildren, with some "taking Mother's side" and others "seeing it Dad's way." Furthermore, divorce within the younger generations can create rather complicated linkages of relationship, especially if, as is likely, remarriage follows. For example, if a seventy-year-old's forty-five-year-old son divorces and remarries a woman with children, relationships with step-grandchildren must be sorted out, not to mention the problem of the former daughter-in-law, who now probably has custody of the "real" grandchildren. Then suppose one of the grandchildren marries, adding a grandson-in-law to the family, but divorces five years and two great-grandchildren later, only to marry a man with a child. Society offers little guidance on appropriate interactions in this maze of divorce-induced relationships.

ON THE ALIENATION OF THE ELDERLY FROM THEIR CHILDREN   One change in American family patterns that has *not* taken place, despite the widespread assumption to the contrary, must be discussed briefly before leaving this consideration of the

45

impact of such changes on care for the elderly. Along with the belief that a sizable segment of America's elderly are institutionalized (in fact, only about 5 percent are in institutions at any given time),[30] the most persistent misapprehensions about the elderly in this country are that families no longer provide much assistance to older members and that aged persons live out their last years in alienation and isolation from their children. Although these widely held beliefs provide some of the favorite targets of those who want to lash out at contemporary America's "ageism," the data simply do not support the claims.

The reality of the situation, attested to by many studies, is summarized best by Ethel Shanas, the person who has done the most to dispel these "social myths," as she calls them:

> In contemporary society, the family persists as a major source of help to the elderly even in those areas where the assistance of outside agencies is undoubtedly necessary and useful.[31]

> Old people are not rejected by their families nor are they alienated from their children. Further, where old people have no children, a principle of family substitution seems to operate and brothers, sisters, nephews and nieces often fulfill the roles and assume the obligations of children. The truly isolated old person, despite his or her prominence in the media, is a rarity in the United States.[32]

Working from national probability samples, Shanas found that four out of five Americans over sixty-five have living children; half of these have one or two children, and the other half have three or more. Although the number of older people who live with their children has declined considerably (from 36 percent in 1957 to 18 percent in 1975), in 1975 three-fourths of the elderly with children lived either with a child or within thirty minutes of a child. Even more significantly, 53 percent of older parents had seen one of their children within one day of their interview, and 77 percent within one week. Only one in ten had *not* seen at least one of their children for a month or more.[33]

A final aspect of the "alienation myth" holds that because of the development of large human service bureaucracies, families no longer want to care for elderly members. This generalization also fails to stand up under the weight of the data. Michael Smyer, citing a classic study of the U.S. General Accounting Office, points out that among the elderly who need the greatest care, four-fifths of such care was provided by relatives and friends. He then concludes, "The GAO's results are perhaps the best-documented in a series of studies that have produced a consistent set of findings—family members are a major source of support for impaired elderly in the United States."[34]

Other clinical evidence and sociological research consistently indicate that adult children do not "dump" aged parents into institutions. As Elaine Brody summarizes the research:

> Studies of the paths leading to institutional care have shown that placing an elderly relative is the last, rather than the first, resort of families. In general, they have exhausted all other alternatives, endured severe personal, social and economic stress in the process, and made the final decision with the utmost reluctance.[35]

To refute the "myth" that the elderly are rejected by their families, however, in no way obviates the very real need for addressing the ethical issues relating to aging and obligations to the elderly from the perspective of the Christian faith. Social research in aging demonstrates that in all Western countries the family plays an important role in old age. Even in the face of cultural changes tending to introduce governmental agencies into areas traditionally the province of the family, the continuing importance of the

47

family may be largely attributable to the underlying strength of the biblical ethic of family responsibility and concern for the elderly. As changes continue and perhaps even accelerate, Christians have the task of seeing that further erosion in this ethic does not occur.

Furthermore, despite the refutation of the myths of lack of care for the elderly by their children and of their alienation from those children, the current situation is hardly cause for unqualified optimism on the part of the aged, especially in light of changes in governmental policy to be considered below. For example, Stephen Crystal points out that when it comes to concrete forms of help for aged parents, such as financial assistance, shared housing, or personal care of the infirm elderly, "it appears that the extended family role has, in fact, undergone significant change, and that to some extent there has been a shift from family to government responsibility as benefits to the aged have grown."[36] Specifically, few Americans today—young *or* old—think that children should be financially responsible for their parents: In 1974 only slightly over 10 percent of the respondents in a national survey considered children an appropriate source of income for elderly parents (interestingly, the elderly themselves were most negative toward filial responsibility in this area [7 percent] and those under 40 most positive [13 percent]); in 1957, 52.5 percent said children should support their aged parents. Private pensions and Social Security were responsible for the bulk of the shift in expectations.

Practice reflects these attitudes: Financial assistance from family members has almost ceased as a significant source of income for older people. Surveys from 1974 and 1981 indicate that fewer than 1 percent of the elderly receive their major financial support from children or other relatives, and that only 5 percent receive enough help to list as "income" at all. Of those who did receive assistance from their children, fewer than one in five thought this an appropriate and desirable situation. In fact, according to their own reports, the elderly are twice as likely to *give* financial help to their children as to *get* it from them, and this direction of transfer holds even among the lowest income groups.

Many observers of the situation of the elderly in contemporary America nonetheless would agree with Marvin B. Sussman's assertion: "The family and its extended kin will become more important to the elderly as a relational, caring, and economic supporting system in this and the remaining decade of the twentieth century."[37] Crystal's less than sanguine conclusion, however, warrants notice by those who think the family will automatically take up the slack in support of the elderly if other sources dry up: "Clearly, the family can no longer be counted on to fill the gaps in income programs. . . . If Social Security and private pensions do not fill the bill, it is unlikely that the family will come back out of the woodwork to provide for the aged."[38] Perhaps the message here is that Christians must give serious consideration to "coming out of the woodwork" in various ways if the elderly are to be provided for.

Changing Government Policies

The difficulties addressed by this book go far deeper than partisan politics, but the impact upon the elderly of certain recent actions of the federal government requires a brief comment. The neoconservatism that has asserted itself during the 1980s has led to a number of policies that reduce the government's role in social services for all ages. The message from Washington contained in the so-called "New Federalism" is clearly that "entitlement" to government assistance is an increasingly tenuous claim. Instead, the presupposition that underlies so much contemporary thought and action in general—that individual worth derives from one's productivity or contribution to society—has become the predominant value in government policy-making as far as social services are concerned.

Those who are able to produce and contribute are valued and rewarded. A number of social policies, however (e.g., mandatory—or at least highly expected—retirement and age-segregated housing and activities), force older people out of productive activity at an age when many still have a great deal to offer. A particularly vicious circle is thus created: Society rewards productivity; it renders the elderly unproductive (unnecessarily so, in many cases); it then complains that because the elderly are unproductive and do not contribute to the well-being of society (economically, that is), they are of little value and do not deserve to be a "drain" upon the nation's resources by "receiving" without commensurate "giving."

Of course, one cannot deny that a basis in *fact* exists for one aspect of the government's position: The elderly do use certain resources in a much larger proportion than younger age groups do. Health care is the most obvious case. In 1984, for example, those over 65 comprised 12 percent of the population but incurred 31 percent of the costs for personal medical services, and people over 65 use (in dollars) over three times the health care services of those under 65. Expenditures in 1984 were $4,202 for each person over 65 and $1,300 for each person under 65.[39] Furthermore, U.S. Census Bureau economists estimate that by 1990 the federal government will be spending $12 billion dollars annually to provide care for those over 85 alone. Because of the projected growth spurt in this segment of the population, this cost is expected to reach $34 billion by the year 2000, more than federal expenditures for any other group and twice the increase for any other class of beneficiaries.[40] That a basis in *fact* exists for the attitude toward the elderly outlined above, however, does not answer the *value* question that is the real concern of this book.

Furthermore, in 1983 the federal government, saying that it was only clarifying that state family-responsibility statutes do not conflict with federal policy, declared that Medicaid (a federal program administered by states to aid the poor with health care costs) gives states the right to require adult children to assist in the support of their elderly parents. The practice has not become widespread, but as the burden of Medicaid upon state budgets continues to grow, it is likely that efforts will increase to enact and enforce such a policy.[41] At any rate, the evidence indicates that for the foreseeable future, economic realities and governmental policy shifts will combine to cause increasing responsibility for older people to fall upon their families. At the same time, as discussed above, a noteworthy decrease has occurred among both old and young in the number who think that children have a financial obligation to their aged parents: Whereas in the mid-fifties around 50 percent felt such an obligation to exist, by the mid-seventies only 10 percent did. One must ask where the elderly are to turn for support if neither the government nor their children wish to assume responsibility for them.

Once again, something of a vicious circle appears to have been created. Although public opinion surveys show an increase in approval of coresidence (parents who live with adult children), the actual incidence of the practice has declined markedly during this century. The explanation seems to be that these trends result primarily from changes in public funding for old age assistance (especially Social Security and Supplemental Security Income), which have led to greater financial independence on the part of the aged. Because living in a household headed by one's child has traditionally connoted dependence, many more aged parents translated their enhanced financial independence

51

into "residential independence," with consequently less reliance on their children for support and assistance. At the same time, of course, their dependence on *public* benefits has increased greatly. As the New Federalism continues to work toward the reduction of public funding for the elderly (which made possible the move toward independence in the first place), they will need to turn elsewhere for the support they no longer can obtain from the government. The past half-century (and especially the past two decades) of public funding, however, have undermined the most logical and certainly the traditional source of support, namely, the family. As the country struggles through this time of rethinking priorities and reducing public funding of human services, reconsideration of traditional ties and responsibilities within families appears to be a crucial undertaking.

Writing in 1979 (before the shift in policy under consideration here), Ethel Shanas concludes her article, "The Family as a Social Support System in Old Age," by asserting that "as families become less able to fulfill the helper role vis-à-vis their aged members they will seek to change and modify the bureaucratic system so that it meets the needs of the elderly in a way more satisfying to both old people and their kin."[42] Given the current political climate, such changes and modifications will not come easily.

The Narcissistic Society

One further change in American society that demands consideration in this context is the widely remarked movement toward greater individualism and self-gratification. Where basic survival needs are met, attention can turn from the struggle for mere existence to the "higher" needs of "self-actualization," a quest that unfortunately tends in this society to take the form of pleasure-, amusement-, and power-seeking. Christopher Lasch has called the result of this movement the "culture of narcissism" and aptly describes the current mood: "Americans have retreated to purely personal preoccupations. . . . To live for the moment is the prevailing passion—to live for yourself, not for your predecessors or posterity." One result is that "we are fast losing the sense of historical continuity, the sense of belonging to a succession of generations originating in the past and stretching into the future."[43] The sense of discontinuity, of isolation from a grand procession of life marching through history, is captured well by Tom Wolfe's comment on contemporary religiosity: "Most people, historically, have *not* lived their lives as if thinking, 'I have only one life to live.' Instead they have lived as if they are living their ancestors' lives and their offspring's lives."[44]

Lasch makes explicit part of the relevance of this discussion to this book when he observes, "In a society that dreads old age and death, aging holds a special terror for those who fear dependence and whose self-esteem requires the admiration usually reserved for youth, beauty, celebrity, or charm." Because the narcissistic personality is not able to find reassurance in "identification with historical continuity," the person cannot accept that the coveted qualities that alone seem to be the source of individual worth now belong exclusively to the young.[45]

Thus lacking a sense of true personal value, the contemporary narcissist must receive the admiration of others in order to maintain self-esteem: "His apparent freedom from family ties and institutional constraints does not free him to stand alone or to glory in his individuality. . . . For the narcissist, the world is a mirror."[46] The comic strip "Bloom County" illustrates the point well when Milo tries to dissuade the penguin Opus from having a "nose job." In response to Opus's challenge to consider "what Barbra Streisand would be with a small nose," Milo says, "A NOBODY!" Opus's rejoinder, "Yes, but an *attractive* nobody," prompts Milo's appropriate judgment, "A metaphor for this generation if I've ever heard one."

A number of contemporary writers on aging illustrate this trend quite clearly. Cohen and Gans, for example, demonstrate one way that self-centeredness (especially widespread in much current writing about the relationship between adult children and their aged parents) can affect the elderly:

> The simple truth, however, is that there are no moral answers to these problems. It is a terrible mistake to think only in such terms. The overall answers you must struggle to find for yourself have to reflect a balance between the needs of your parents for care and attention and your own needs for living your life with minimal guilt and maximum peace of mind.[47]

Up to a point, of course, the position is unarguable. Adult children must consider their own needs. From a Christian perspective, nonetheless, a significant question arises about whether or not the balance has swung too far away from "the needs of your parents" toward "your own needs." Furthermore, for those who affirm that God is sovereign over all of life (and certainly over that portion of it that concerns human relationships, especially within families), can the assertion that "there are no moral answers to these problems" be accepted as such a "simple truth" (or a truth at all)? It appears not, unless one is prepared to argue that morality has no place in so central an issue in our society as the care of the elderly.

Later, Cohen and Gans assert that "being a thoughtful, sensitive son or daughter should never be incompatible with the right to preserve your own happiness without the burden of excessive responsibilities."[48] Clearly at issue here are fundamental value assumptions: What constitutes "happiness," and what "right" does one have to it where the happiness of others is also involved? When do responsibilities become "excessive" or even a "burden" at all? Answers to the questions will differ markedly, given one's basic value system. For this reason the underlying values demand not mere assumption and assertion as givens, but serious consideration and explicit examination.

Such, then, are some of the major issues facing the United States as the population evolves in a direction unprecedented in human history—toward a society in which virtually everyone lives to "a ripe old age" (in fact, to an age greater than that attained by most people who have ever lived), and certainly to a healthier old age. The nation has a great deal of thinking to do about how to cope with this new situation, and many of the problems raised do not lend themselves to simple solutions. Writing twenty-five years ago, Michael Harrington put the issue clearly in words that warrant hearing again today:

> Perhaps the most important thing that must be done with regard to the aged is to change our operative philosophy about them. We have . . . a "storage bin" philosophy in America. We "maintain" the aged; we give them the gift of life, but we take away the possibility of dignity. Perhaps one of the most basic reasons why America has such problems with its elderly men and women is that America really doesn't care about them.[49]

As difficult as this problem is for Americans in general, for Christians the issues are even more complex, for reasons that are probably apparent to most readers and that will be addressed explicitly in the rest of this book. In addition to all the questions that everyone in this country faces, Christians must confront very specific teachings in their religion about appropriate treatment of the elderly and must ask if such views are tenable in the radically different demographic milieu of today.

What should the Christian's attitude (and action) in this

area be? It has been said that Christian decision-making about ethical issues requires two elements: faith and facts. This chapter has contributed some of the *facts* necessary for informed reflection by providing information about the current situation of the elderly. In addition, however, the position of the Christian with regard to the elderly will be determined by the view one holds of aging itself and the commitment one has to foster a just and a fulfilling life for all members of society. These are fundamentally matters of *faith.* For the Christian, the primary source of information on matters of belief and practice is the basic writings of the faith—the Old and the New Testaments—and to these documents the attention of this book now turns.

NOTES

1. Maggie Kuhn, "Aging—Challenge to the Whole Society," in Dieter Hessel, ed., *Empowering Ministry in an Ageist Society* (New York: The Program Agency, United Presbyterian Church, U.S.A., 1981), pp. 3-4.

2. Joseph A. Kuypers and Vern L. Bengston, "Toward Competence in the Older Family," in Timothy H. Brubaker, ed., *Family Relationships in Later Life* (Beverly Hills: Sage Publications, 1983), p. 221.

3. Stephen Z. Cohen and Bruce Michael Gans, *The Other Generation Gap: The Middle-aged and Their Aging Parents* (Chicago: Follett, 1978), p. 3.

4. The statistics in this section come from several sources. Most are taken from a very useful pamphlet entitled "A Profile of Older Americans: 1986," prepared by the Program Resources Department, American Association of Retired Persons, and the Administration on Aging, U.S. Department of Health and Human Services, based upon data compiled by Donald G. Fowles of the Administration on Aging, pp. 1-2. Helpful historical data can be found in David H. Fischer, *Growing Old in America,* expanded ed. (New York: Oxford University Press, 1978), especially the appendix.

5. In her preface to a volume that she edited (*Aging and Income: Programs and Prospects for the Elderly,* The Gerontological Society, special publication no. 4 [New York: Human Sciences Press, 1978], p. 11), Barbara Rieman Herzog points to this "lull" in the growth rate of the elderly to make a significant point: "Thus during the next quarter century we have a breather—time to establish the policies which will have such an impact when the retiree bulge finally occurs between 2010 and 2040."

6. Although this book focuses on the United States, it is noteworthy that worldwide, of all the people in human history who have reached the age of sixty-five, *one-half* are alive today.

7. William F. May, "Who Cares for the Elderly?" *Hastings Center Report* 12 (December 1982): 31.

8. Robert Butler, *Why Survive? Being Old in America* (New York: Harper & Row, 1975), p. xi.

9. See, e.g., Albert Rosenfeld, *Prolongevity* (New York: Alfred A. Knopf, 1976); and Joel Kurtzman and Phillip Gordon, *No More Dying: The Conquest of Aging and the Extension of Human Life* (New York: Dell, 1977). Dr. Edward L. Schneider, deputy director of the National Institute on Aging ("No cure for aging, MD says," *Miami Herald*, May 16, 1985), concluded after an extensive review of the research that medical science has no valid method for slowing the aging process or for increasing the life span (i.e., the maximum age a human being can attain). In fact, although life *expectancy* has increased from around 45 to 75 since 1900, the life span of about 115 years has not changed much over the last century. Schneider did emphasize that people can do a great deal to make these extra years healthier and therefore, presumably, happier.

10. The statistics in this paragraph are from Fischer, *Growing Old in America*, pp. 142-46, 279.

11. Fischer, *Growing Old in America*, p. 139.

12. John Naisbitt, *Megatrends: Ten New Directions Transforming Our Lives*, rev. ed. (New York: Warner Books, 1984), p. 7.

13. Alvin Toffler, *The Third Wave* (New York: Bantam Books, 1980), p. 216.

14. Naisbitt, *Megatrends*, p. 18.

15. Leo W. Simmons, *The Role of the Aged in Primitive Society* (New Haven, Conn.: Yale University Press, 1945), p. 79.

16. Stephen Crystal (*America's Old Age Crisis* [New York: Basic Books, 1982], pp. 5-6) points out that in 1982, twenty-seven of every one hundred federal dollars were spent on benefits for the elderly. Projections (assuming *no* increase in benefits) put the same cost at 35 percent of the federal budget in the year 2000 and 65 percent in 2025. Currently, all levels of government spend only one-third as much on children and youth (including education) as on the aged.

17. Irving Rosow, "Status and Role Change Through the Life Cycle," in Robert H. Binstock and Ethel Shanas, eds., *Handbook of Aging and the Social Sciences*, 2d ed. (New York: Van Nostrand Reinhold, 1985), pp. 62-93. The material in the text comes from pp. 71-73.

18. Elaine Brody, " 'Women in the Middle' and Family Help to Older People," *Gerontologist* 21 (1981): 474.

19. "Women choose jobs over kids," *Miami Herald*, November 21, 1985.

20. These factors and their interrelationships are explored thoroughly in Wendy H. Baldwin and Christine W. Nord, "Delayed Childbearing in the U.S.: Facts and Fictions," *Population Bulletin* 39 (November 1984). Unless otherwise noted, the data in the next three paragraphs come from this source.

21. "Number of unwed-couple households drops," *Miami Herald*, November 20, 1985.

22. William F. Pratt, William D. Mosher, Christine A. Bachrach, and Marjorie C. Horn, "Understanding U. S. Fertility: Findings from the National Survey of Family Growth, Cycle III," *Population Bulletin* 39 (December 1984): 8-9. Alvin Toffler's research (*The Third Wave*, p. 213) leads him to foresee an even more significant change, namely, "growth in the number of those consciously choosing

what is coming to be known as a 'child-free' life-style." He cites the observation of James Ramey of the Center for Policy Research that "we are seeing a massive shift from 'child-centered' to 'adult-centered' homes."

23. Shirley H. Rhine, *America's Aging Population: Issues Facing Business and Society*, report no. 785 (New York: The Conference Board, 1980), pp. 13-14.

24. Ethel Shanas, "Older People and Their Families: The New Pioneers," *Journal of Marriage and the Family* 42 (February 1980): 14.

25. Spencer Rich, "Study Says Women Provide Most Home Care for Elderly," *Washington Post*, August 4, 1986.

26. Crystal, *America's Old Age Crisis*, pp. 44-45, 55.

27. Shanas, "New Pioneers," p. 12. The statistics on approval of coresidence come from Crystal, *America's Old Age Crisis*, pp. 46-47, 222.

28. Cited in Timothy H. Brubaker, *Later Life Families* (Beverly Hills: Sage Publications, 1985), p. 20. For details of what is known about divorce and the elderly, see chapter 6 of *Later Life Families* and especially Charles B. Hennon, "Divorce and the Elderly: A Neglected Area of Research," in Brubaker, *Family Relationships*, pp. 149-72.

29. Hennon, "Divorce and the Elderly," in Brubaker, *Family Relationships*, pp. 167-68.

30. This figure is a favorite citation by commentators to demonstrate the extent of misinformation about the elderly among the general public (some surveys, e.g., show respondents estimating as high as 33 percent of people over 65 in institutions). The relatively positive note sounded by the 5 percent institutionalization rate, however, needs to be balanced by Erdman Palmore's observation ("Total Chance of Institutionalization Among the Aged," *Gerontologist* 16 [1976]: 505) that although only one in twenty over 65 is in a nursing home at a particular time, one in *four* will enter an institution at *some* time before his or her death. Furthermore, according to the AARP's "Profile of Older Americans: 1986" (p. 4), the percentage institutionalized increases significantly with age: From a low of 2 percent for those 65-74, the number increases to 7 per cent for those 75-84 and to 23 percent for those 85 and older.

31. Ethel Shanas, "The Family as a Social Support System in Old Age," *Gerontologist* 19 (1979): 170.

32. Ethel Shanas, "Social Myth as Hypothesis: The Case of the Family Relations of Old People," *Gerontologist* 19 (1979): 3-4.

33. Shanas, "Social Myth," pp. 6-7, and "The Family," p. 173.

34. Michael Smyer, "Aging and Social Policy: Contrasting Western Europe and the United States," *Journal of Family Issues* 5 (June 1984): 240.

35. Elaine Brody, *Long-term Care for Older People* (New York: Human Sciences Press, 1977), quoted in Shanas, "Social Myth," p. 8.

36. Crystal, *America's Old Age Crisis*, p. 12. For copious evidence for Crystal's position, see chapter 3 of his book, "The Family Support System," pp. 39-65. The following data are from pp. 56-57.

37. Marvin B. Sussman, "The Family Life of Old People," in Binstock and Shanas, *Handbook*, p. 415.

38. Crystal, *America's Old Age Crisis*, pp. 56, 58.

39. "A Profile of Older Americans: 1986," p. 14.

40. Mike Toner, "Big Cost Hike Predicted in Care for Aged," *Miami Herald*, May 27, 1984.

41. Daniel Callahan, "What Do Children Owe Elderly Parents?" *Hastings Center Report* 15 (April 1985): 32. On p. 33 he points out that "some twenty-six

states at present have statutes that can require children to provide financial support for needy parents," though such laws are "erratically administered, difficult to implement, and of doubtful financial value."

42. Shanas, "The Family," p. 174.

43. Christopher Lasch, *The Culture of Narcissism: American Life in an Age of Diminishing Expectations* (New York: W. W. Norton, 1978), pp. 4-5. See also Aaron Stern, *Me: The Narcissistic American* (New York: Ballantine Books, 1979). The use of the term by Lasch and others may not do justice to the complexity of the psychoanalytical concept of narcissism. Such considerations, however, are not the concern of this book, and the notion of a "narcissistic" society describes quite well the phenomena discussed here, namely, the increasing tendency of contemporary Americans to think first of themselves and the fulfillment of their own desires, to have little sense of continuity with past and future generations (and thus little feeling of gratitude toward those who have gone before and of obligation toward those who follow), and to base judgments of personal value on external, superficial, and therefore ultimately temporal personal characteristics.

44. Tom Wolfe, "The 'Me' Decade," *Harper's* (October 1975): 40, quoted in Lasch, *Narcissism,* pp. 6-7.

45. Lasch, *Narcissism,* p. 41.

46. Ibid, p. 10.

47. Cohen and Gans, *The Other Generation Gap,* p. 12; cf. their statement cited in note 3 above. Virtually all of the books that deal specifically with this question share the underlying point of view of Cohen and Gans, though perhaps without being quite so explicit about the priority of the children's concerns. The matter is not a simple one to resolve, as chapter 5 will show, and well may be the central issue of this whole topic.

48 Ibid., p. 32.

49. Michael Harrington, *The Other America: Poverty in the United States* (Baltimore: Penguin Books, 1962), p. 118.

AGING AND THE ELDERLY IN THE OLD TESTAMENT

CHAPTER TWO

This chapter will survey some of the major Old Testament statements concerning aging and obligations toward the elderly. Special attention will be given to the central teaching on this subject, the fifth commandment of the Decalogue. A study of biblical sources about aging and the elderly, however, cannot examine only explicit statements or even illustrative stories. In both the Old and the New Testaments, direct references must be supplemented by, and in some cases interpreted in light of, a more general understanding of the biblical faith and witness to God's perceived purposes in human history. Preliminary to discovering what the Old Testament has to say specifically concerning attitudes about aging and obligations toward the elderly, consideration of two of the crucial anthropological affirmations of the Hebrew Bible will prove helpful to this inquiry.

Basic Anthropological Affirmations

"The Image of God"

The belief that human beings are created "in the image of God" has considerable influence on attitudes about aging in the Old Testament, and this doctrine also colors the understanding of obligations toward the aged. Of course, numerous interpretations of the meaning of "the image of God" have been suggested. These range from a literal reading of the Hebrew terms "image" and "likeness" (i.e., that human beings are in some way a physical representation of God) to a completely spiritual view (i.e., that the image refers to the human capacity for reason, self-transcendence, freedom of choice, moral responsibility, and the like). In Genesis 5:3, Seth is also described as being "in the image of " his father Adam, a resemblance that clearly includes a physical component. Many scholars today hold the view that the author[1] meant, by employing the term "in the image of God," that human beings are God's representatives on earth in much the same way that the statues of earthly kings remind the inhabitants of conquered lands of their rulers (cf. Dan. 3:1-7). Humans thus acquire considerable authority and worth merely by virtue of being God's representatives.

Indeed, both creation accounts make it quite clear that human beings are the crown of God's creative activity. In its more narrative fashion, J depicts the human being as Yahweh's first and clearly special creature, upon whom the inbreathing of God's own "breath" bestowed life (Gen. 2:7; significantly, in Hebrew the word for breath also means

61

"spirit"). In addition, the animals were brought to the man to be given names, in Hebrew thought a symbolic indication of the human's superiority and dominance over them. Psalm 8 well summarizes the place that human beings hold in the Genesis creation accounts: "Yet thou hast made [the human being] little less than God, and dost crown him with glory and honor. Thou hast given him dominion over the works of thy hands; thou hast put all things under his feet" (vv. 5-6).

An essential and significant reason for this lofty position is a characteristic unique to humanity, expressed in the idea that human nature consists of a psychophysical unity. Unlike the view held by most Westerners as a legacy from dualistic Greek thought (enhanced by Cartesian philosophy), in Hebrew thought the body and the soul were not separate entities only accidentally cohering. Rather, they were interdependent elements, both of which had to exist for there to be a human being. The body was thus an essential part of human nature; in fact, for ancient Hebrew religion there simply was no person without a body, as the absence (at least until the post-exilic period) of a concept of personal, individual immortality attests. This unifying emphasis can serve as a needed corrective for the devaluation of the body evident throughout most of Christian history, a devaluation that has reappeared in various forms in some contemporary writing about the universal phenomenon of aging.

By presenting humans as being created in the image of God, however, the Priestly creation account was conveying something of importance equal to the significance of the body, namely, that human beings are *more than* merely bodies, just as the ancient Hebrews unquestionably conceived God to be far more than physical in nature. Because the body was the outward manifestation of the total person, creation in the image of God meant that human beings shared in some sense those spiritual powers of God that transcend the body. Without entering the debate about precisely what those qualities are, one surely can say that creation in God's image means at least that humans are created with a capacity to relate to God—to know God—in a way different from any other of God's creatures.[2] Thus the discussion comes full circle to the affirmation that humankind is indeed the "crown of God's creation," sharing in some sense in God's own likeness.

Actually, for the purposes of this study the *precise* meaning of "the image of God" is not crucial. What is significant and what must be remembered is that according to biblical accounts, human creation in the image of God appears to be the ultimate source of the value and the dignity of all human beings, whatever other characteristics one may attribute to them. Indeed, if human beings are created in the image of God, they never can be valued solely according to *physical* attributes or even bodily integrity.

The Importance of Community

The early chapters of Genesis yield another important fact about the Hebrew concept of human nature and God's intentions for his human creatures: In God's eyes, the *solitary* human being simply does not exist. Humans are considered only within and as part of a larger group. Both creation accounts clearly state God's intention that his human creatures exist in relationship with each other. Genesis 1, in its more abstract, theological language, simply affirms that "he created *them*" (v. 27*c*), leaving no doubt that humanity exists in community. Genesis 2 more picturesquely states, "It is not good that the man should be alone" (v. 18*a*), again attesting to the fact that only as human beings exist in relationship with other human beings (the animals were not adequate "partners" for the man) do they find and fulfill the potential for which they were created. Thus separation from one's community was reason for complaint (cf. Job 19:13-19; Jer. 15:15-18, esp. v. 17), and excommunication was tantamount to death (cf. Ex. 12:15, 19; Lev. 17:4; Num. 19:20). Indeed, community is so essential for humanity that, unlike today, the real theological issue for the Old Testament was not the creation of community from disparate individuals but the discovery of individual worth and responsibility within the community.

Human beings were created for community, then, and it was only because of disobedience to God that the community was broken. As Genesis 3 graphically portrays, human pride led to a sundering of the relationship with God, with self, with others, and with nature. Furthermore, the centrality of community created a collective responsibility that suggests that guilt may be ascribed to an individual merely as a member of the community even without direct personal involvement in the misdeed. The fact that all the descendants of Adam and Eve had to pay the consequences of the first couple's sin is a vivid depiction of this collective responsibility. Indeed, the entire remainder of the Bible is arguably a report of the mutual effort of God and humankind to restore the harmony that the first disobedience destroyed, and both the lingering effects of the disharmony and the reconciliation that God has offered will play important roles later in this inquiry.

Although not often made explicit (and perhaps not frequently a conscious thought of the authors), the theme of human creation in the image of God is reflected throughout the Old Testament—if not always in the practice of Old Testament characters, then at least in the laws. Recognition of the crucial importance of community is much more evident. The rest of this chapter explores the ways in which these central anthropological concepts of Hebrew religion affected attitudes and obligations toward aging and the elderly.

Attitudes Toward Aging

What does the Old Testament say about the process of aging itself? What does it mean to get old and to be old? Consideration of these questions will lead to the discovery of a frank and honest assessment of aging that acknowledges both positive and negative aspects, with no attempt to gloss over the realities or to ignore the facts.

The Inevitability of Aging

In general, the Old Testament affirms that aging is *inevitable* and as such something to be accepted as part of God's plan for human life. This view is closely related to the Hebrew Scriptures' understanding of mortality. Because human beings are earthly creatures (Gen. 2:7), they are mortal: They will live a certain length of time (Ps. 39:4; 90:10) and then will return to the dust from which they came (Gen. 3:19; Job 10:9; Ps. 90:3; Eccles. 12:7). As David approached death, he told Solomon, "I am about to go the way of all the earth" (1 Kings 2:2; cf. Josh. 23:14; Is. 40:7-8; 2 Sam. 14:14). Birth and death are merely the two extremes of human existence, the bookends of life, as it were. Ecclesiastes expresses this thought in poetry: "For everything there is a season, and a time for every matter under heaven: a time to be born, and a time to die" (3:1-2). Verse 11 affirms that this scheme is part of the plan of God, who "has made everything beautiful in its time." Thus Lloyd Bailey can conclude:

> From the point of view of ancient Israel's canonical faith, death is the natural consummation of biological life. Rather than a dismal interruption of life in old age, mortality is the proper boundary for creaturely existence. It has been programmed into human biology from the beginning of creation and is evident in each life from the moment of birth.[3]

65

Applying this point of view to the more specific concern of this study, aging and old age come to be seen simply as another stage of the human journey from birth to death. As with death, the Old Testament accepts relatively easily a universal in human experience—growing older—universal, that is, unless one is deprived of the opportunity to do so. It is the danger of dying *prematurely* that agitated the ancient Hebrews, not the "problem" of losing one's youth and growing old. Among the types of death that the Old Testament considers "bad" or "evil," then, one finds the death that is premature, that prevents a human *life* from reaching its full potential. Referring to Abraham at the time of his death as "an old man and full of years," Gerhard von Rad asserts, "The expression reveals that one felt only an early or an 'evil' death as a judgment from God."[4] When the thirty-nine-year-old Hezekiah thought he was going to die, he said, "In the noontide of my days I must depart. . . . My dwelling is plucked up and removed from me like a shepherd's tent; like a weaver I have rolled up my life; he cuts me off from the loom" (Is. 38:10, 12). The sense of incompleteness, of unfulfilled potential, fairly leaps out of this lament.

The view that early death is bad contains a definite element of judgment (cf. 1 Sam. 2:32), especially in the Wisdom literature. For example, Elihu asserted to Job that the "godless . . . die in youth, and their life ends in shame" (Job 36:13-14); and Proverbs 10:27 bluntly warns, "The fear of the Lord prolongs life, but the years of the wicked will be short" (cf. Prov. 3:1-2—"My son, do not forget my teaching, but let your heart keep my commandments; for length of days and years of life and abundant welfare will they give you"; also Prov. 12:28).

The obvious corollary of this understanding that a premature death is bad is that death at an advanced age is good, indeed, is a sign of favor and blessing from Yahweh.

In a catalogue of blessings that God will bestow on those whom he chastens—including such an obvious desire as knowing that "your descendants shall be many, and your offspring as the grass of the earth" (Job 5:25)—Eliphaz assured Job that he would experience the death of the righteous: "You shall come to your grave in ripe old age, as a shock of grain comes up to the threshing floor in its season" (Job 5:26; cf. Job 42:17 for the fulfillment of the promise). Psalm 91 affirms that "because he cleaves to me in love . . . with long life I will satisfy him, and show him my salvation (vv. 14, 16); and Psalm 92 says of "the righteous" that "they still bring forth fruit in old age, they are ever full of sap and green" (vv. 12, 14). Proverbs 16:31 is very explicit: "A hoary head is a crown of glory; it is gained in a righteous life."

The death of Abraham, which seems almost to be the Old Testament model for death as Yahweh intends it for his human creatures, depicts the same attitude. As he had been promised years before—"you shall go to your fathers in peace; you shall be buried in a good old age" (Gen. 15:15)—so it was at the end of Abraham's 175 years: He "died in a good old age, an old man and full of years, and was gathered to his people" (Gen. 25:8; cf. 35:29; 1 Chron. 29:28; 2 Chron. 24:15).

In Old Testament thought, then, old age, though perhaps lamentable (for reasons to appear shortly), was not something one dreaded or resented as an intrusion into God's intended purpose and design for human existence; rather it was something one accepted, if not welcomed. The reason is simple: Length of days was a sign of God's favor and blessing, and death "in a good old age," as "an old man and full of years," was the reward for righteousness. Obviously, it was impossible to die "full of years" without experiencing old age! Indeed, in the eschatological restoration that Yahweh would accomplish, the ideal life would not be endless but would include a considerable span of time that one must classify as "old age": "For behold, I create new heavens and a new earth. . . . No more shall there be in it an infant that lives but a few days, or an old man who does not fill out his days, for the child shall die a hundred years old" (Is. 65:17, 20).

Rolf Knierim provides a fitting conclusion to this look at the Hebrew Scriptures' acceptance of the inevitability of aging (and a sharp contrast to contemporary views) when he points out, "Aging and old age are not periods of transition between life and death, and not at all the first phase of death. They belong to life."[5]

The Loss of Vitality Associated with Aging

Aging then is inevitable according to Hebrew thought, and partly for that reason and partly because long life is a sign of God's blessing, one should not resent or unduly dread growing old. Typically, however, the Old Testament does not sugarcoat the realities of human existence but honestly depicts life as men and women experience it. Such is certainly the case when it comes to aging: The Hebrew Scriptures explicitly recognize the loss of vitality and powers that accompanies becoming old, and the diminution of quality of life that this loss brings about receives clear expression. Significantly, however, the diminution—no matter how many problems it might occasion—never renders life unbearable or not worth living (see Ps. 71 for a classic statement of this point).

Nonetheless, the Old Testament clearly sets forth the losses of aging, and the contrast expressed in Proverbs 20:29 provides a keynote expression of this (though not without some ambivalence): "The glory of young men is their strength, but the beauty of old men is their gray hair."

Beauty perhaps is to be desired, but few people would consider the trade of strength for gray hair very desirable (cf. Hos. 7:9, where gray hairs, this time "sprinkled upon him, and he knows it not," are a sign of *weakness* resulting from forsaking Yahweh and seeking help from other gods and nations).

The general debilitation associated with aging finds illustration in a number of places. For example, Numbers 4:3 (v. 23 also) sets the age limits for a Levite's "active duty" in the tent of meeting between thirty (later lowered—cf. Num. 8:24; 1 Chron. 23:24) and fifty (never raised, though "retired" Levites later were allowed to "minister to their brethren" but must "serve no more"—Num. 8:25-26). Apparently a person of fifty was considered no longer able to perform the services required (described in Num. 4:4-33), many of which demanded quite a bit of physical strength.

Similarly, Leviticus 27:1-8 presents a "rate schedule" that sets a monetary value by which one could redeem individuals consecrated to God's service (cf. 1 Sam. 1:11); presumably productivity determined value. For males, the values were as follows: one month to five years of age—five shekels; five to twenty years—twenty shekels; twenty to sixty years—fifty shekels; and over sixty years—fifteen shekels. Apparently Hebrew society expected a sharp drop in one's ability to work after sixty, perhaps the standard "retirement age" in ancient Israel. Interestingly, the corresponding values for females are three, ten, thirty, and ten shekels— figures that reflect the lower valuation of females in Hebrew society but, significantly, also recognize that the *older* woman is of greater relative value in a traditional society than the older man.

In a number of other places the Hebrew Scriptures recognize the losses resulting from aging. In Genesis 27:1-4, for example, Isaac had no illusions about growing old, and the narrative comments in particular upon the blindness often associated with old age (as elsewhere: Gen. 27:21; 48:10; 1 Sam. 3:2; 4:15). Indeed, it is noteworthy when weakness of eyesight and loss of general physical strength do *not* accompany aging (e.g., Deut. 34:7—"Moses was a hundred and twenty years old when he died; his eye was not dim, nor his natural force abated"). Various texts also acknowledge the waning of other senses and powers, such as the woman's inability to conceive (Gen. 18:13); the clumsiness of old age (as well as obesity!—1 Sam. 4:18); poor circulation and loss of sexual desire and/or potency (1 Kings 1:1-4); problems with the feet (1 Kings 15:23); and a general loss of sensual acuity and the attendant pleasures of life (2 Sam. 19:35). Psalm 71, an old man's prayer for divine deliverance, refers to "spent strength" (v. 9) and "many sore troubles" (v. 20), expresses fear of being "cast . . . off in the time of old age" and "forsaken," and perceives conspiratorial plotting as "my enemies speak concerning me [and] consult together" (vv. 9-10). Here is a frank presentation of not only the physical losses of aging but also some of the psychological problems as well.[6] Zechariah 8:4-5, describing the restored Zion, draws a sharp contrast between the children playing in the streets and the "old men and old women" who will "sit in the streets of Jerusalem, each with staff in hand for very age."

Two other passages also present the same realistic attitude toward the losses of aging. The first is the account of the eighty-year-old Barzillai's tactful refusal of King David's offer to care for him in Jerusalem as repayment for his help when David was fleeing from Absalom (2 Sam. 19:31-39). Barzillai showed a keen awareness of both the effects of aging and their likely impact upon his enjoyment of the royal palace:

> How many years have I still to live, that I should go up with the king to Jerusalem? I am this day eighty years old; can I

discern what is pleasant and what is not? Can your servant taste what he eats or what he drinks? Can I still listen to the voice of singing men and singing women? Why then should your servant be an added burden to my lord the king? . . . Pray let your servant return, that I may die in my own city near the grave of my father and my mother.

He then suggested a younger man as more suited to enjoy the king's generosity, a further recognition of the advantages of youth over age for certain activities and pleasures.[7]

Another explicit depiction of the unpleasant side of aging, even more pessimistic and discouraging, is the famous allegory of Ecclesiastes 12, which opens by calling old age "the evil days . . . when you will say, 'I have no pleasure in them' " (v. 1). After this frank warning, the author presents in wonderfully metaphorical language (the meaning of all of which is not totally clear) what one should expect (though *not* look forward to)

when the keepers of the house tremble, and the strong men are bent, and the grinders cease because they are few, and those that look through the windows are dimmed, and the doors on the street are shut; . . . the almond tree blossoms, the grasshopper drags itself along and desire fails. (vv. 3-5)

Obviously for Qoheleth the reality of aging, with all the losses it represents, is part of the "vanity of vanities" that human existence is all about.[8]

Despite the Old Testament's rather gloomy—though realistic—picture of the loss of vitality that accompanies aging, exceptions exist. For example, at 85 Caleb asserts, "I am still as strong to this day as I was in the day that Moses sent me; my strength now is as my strength was then" (Josh. 14:11). Also worthy of mention is the scriptural claim that Moses was 80 and Aaron 83 when Yahweh called them to convince Pharaoh to release the Hebrew slaves (Ex. 7:7). And, as pointed out previously, when Deuteronomy states that Moses died at 120, it also affirms that he still possessed all his "natural force" (34:7). Clearly, age in and of itself does not disqualify one from all worthwhile activity, and the Hebrew Scriptures give no indication whatsoever that advancing years in any way diminish "the image of God" within humanity. Certainly Israel believed that God's love and concern for his human creatures continue into old age, as expressed explicitly in Isaiah 46:4, where Yahweh assures Israel, "Even to your old age I am He, and to gray hairs I will carry you." Furthermore, only a chapter later Babylon is condemned because "on the aged you made your yoke exceedingly heavy" (Is. 47:6). Indeed, the honest recognition that the elderly *do* suffer these various losses may have led the Old Testament writers to express such deep concern for their well-being, care, and protection.

Age as a Source of Wisdom

Despite the frank acknowledgment of the losses associated with aging, as in most traditional societies, so in ancient Israel the elderly had a special role and place in the community, as Deuteronomy 32:7 illustrates. Moses was calling the people of Israel to task for their faithlessness to the God who had been ever faithful to them: "Remember the days of old, consider the years of many generations; ask your father, and he will show you; your elders, and they will tell you." For Hebrew religion, the past was indeed the present and the future: *History* was the arena of Yahweh's mighty saving acts, and the community could not ignore or devalue it without grave danger to those whose welfare depended on their relationship to the God of Abraham, Isaac, and Jacob.

Thus if one wanted to know the things that make for

happiness, for success, indeed, for *life*, those who had lived long and experienced much (including frequently the "sacred history" itself) were the best source. Throughout the Old Testament, wisdom worthy of the name is *practical* wisdom, and knowledge is not abstract but concrete, providing guidance about how to act in a certain situation. Thus the authors highly value the chance to learn from those who have accumulated a lifetime of experience in living and strongly frown upon ignoring such an opportunity (cf., e.g., 1 Kings 12:6-20, where Rehoboam ignored the counsel of "the old men" to serve the people and instead listened to the "childish fools"[9] his own age, with the tragic results that the narrator made clear in v. 19: "So Israel has been in rebellion against the house of David to this day"). The Hebrew Scriptures strongly affirm that if society fails to take advantage of what its elders have to offer, in the words of Benjamin Blech, "we are strangers to the accumulated wisdom of personal experience because we chose to make strangers of those who could enlighten us."[10]

Examples of the wisdom attributed to the aged in Hebrew society are numerous throughout the Old Testament. Exodus, for example, depicts Moses—though under Yahweh's special call and quite old himself—as accepting the advice of his father-in-law Jethro, obviously an older man, about the administration of justice (18:13-27). Jeremiah reflected the societal understanding that wisdom is correlated with age when he tried to reject Yahweh's call to prophecy with the demurrer, "Ah, Lord God! Behold, I do not know how to speak, for I am only a youth" (1:6). Clearly, the young Jeremiah assumed that "a prophet to the nations" needed to be older and wiser than he was.[11]

Elihu illustrated the widespread agreement with this point of view at the beginning of his speech in Job by saying, "I am young in years, and you are aged; therefore I was timid and afraid to declare my opinion to you. I said, 'Let days

73

speak, and many years teach wisdom' " (32:6-7). Of course, he then questioned the facile acceptance of this perspective: "It is not the old that are wise, nor the aged that understand what is right. Therefore I say, 'Listen to me; let me also declare my opinion' " (vv. 9-10). Yet even as he exhibited youthful brashness, he demonstrated by his initial deference his acknowledgment of his proper place, and he challenged only what was clearly the accepted view of his society.

Further testimony to the wisdom of the older generation comes from the fact that it was the *elders* who sat at the city gates and pronounced judgment in various judicial cases. This role suggests that their years had given them the experience to make difficult decisions fairly (Deut. 21:1-9, 18-21; 22:13-21; 25:5-10; Num. 11:16-17; Ruth 4:1-12; Ps. 107:32; Jer. 26:17-19). G. Henton Davies likens the authority of elders in a clan, tribe, or local community to that which parents wield in a family and concludes, "This fact of age is undoubtedly the true origin of the authority of elders, and is the prerequisite of any official appointments that may be made."[12] On the other hand, as S. H. Blank (among others) points out, "The old man is not necessarily to be equated with the Elder, who occupied an official position in biblical society."[13] Whatever development occurred in the concept of "elder" during Israel's history, the choice of that specific term for the *office* shows an original correlation between age and the particular qualifications for the function, chief among which was the wisdom of experience. Job 12:12 thus expresses well the prevailing opinion of the biblical authors: "Wisdom is with the aged, and under-standing in length of days" (cf. 15:9-10: "What do you know that we do not know? What do you understand that is not clear to us? Both the gray-haired and the aged are among us, older than your father").

The correlation of wisdom with age, however, is not absolute, as Elihu's speech to Job contended. Although

Elihu did not abandon his earlier acceptance of the priority of age over youth, or the general assumption that "many years teach wisdom," he did enter the appropriate caveat that length of years does not necessarily equal depth of wisdom: "It is not the old that are wise, nor the aged that understand what is right. . . . But it is the spirit in a man, the breath of the Almighty, that makes him understand" (32:8, 9). Of course Elihu, for all his youthful self-confidence and impatience with Job and his three friends, did not produce a very helpful answer either. As much of the preceding discussion has demonstrated, the way in which one lives—that is, whether or not one lives a righteous life—and not simply one's age determines one's true wisdom. Thus the Psalmist can sing, "I understand more than the aged, for I keep thy precepts" (Ps. 119:100), and Qoheleth can warn, "Better is a poor and wise youth than an old and foolish king, who will no longer take advice" (Eccles. 4:13).

Overall, then, the Old Testament considers wisdom that is based on knowledge of Yahweh's saving acts in Israel's history and on accumulation of the experiences of living to be especially associated with the elderly, though the correlation is not absolute. A crucial result of this view, and one of the most important facts to come out of this study, is that the aged are entitled to particular respect and consideration because of their wisdom and special role in society. Thus certain obligations toward the elderly are incumbent upon the younger generation.

Obligations Toward the Elderly

Concern for the Needy

In general, the Old Testament throughout expresses a deep-seated concern for the disadvantaged, the oppressed, and the weak, especially in its legal sections and some of the prophets. Leviticus 19, for example, which presents much of the ethical material of the Holiness Code, contains requirements to leave part of the harvest for gleaners (vv. 9-10), to be fair in various kinds of business dealings (vv. 13, 15, 35-36), to show extra concern for the deaf and the blind (v. 14), to honor the elderly (v. 32, of special interest to this study), and, above all (and underlying all), to "love your neighbor as yourself" (v. 18).

The prophetic utterances of compassion for the poor and the afflicted are well known. Isaiah of Jerusalem, for example, speaks the word of Yahweh to Judah: "Cease to do evil, learn to do good; seek justice, correct oppression; defend the fatherless, plead for the widow" (1:16c-17). In the Servant Songs of Second Isaiah the deaf, the blind, the robbed, the hungry, the thirsty, and the imprisoned are the special recipients of Yahweh's concern (42:7, 18-22; 49:9-10). And Isaiah 61:1-9 (cited by Jesus to interpret his own mission) promises the afflicted, the brokenhearted, the captives, the mourners, the aliens, and the foreigners "everlasting joy." And through Amos, Yahweh declares, "Hear this, you who trample upon the needy, and bring the poor of the land to an end, . . . I will turn your feasts into mourning, and all your songs into lamentation" (8:4, 10; cf. Jer. 7:5-7).

It is important to understand the reason for this concern, common to most religions but strongly developed in ancient Israel: The relationship between God and human beings ultimately determines the relationships *among* human beings. Thus Theodor Vriezen concludes that for the Old Testament

> the relation between man and man is dominated by the relation between man and God . . . ; as Yahweh lives in community with man, man is also linked with his fellowman

by *chesed* (faithfulness). Men linked together by Yahweh are brothers. Israel is a community of brothers. . . . Within this community men must help each other as much as lies within their power. And, like the relation between God and man, that between man and man is also personal throughout.[14]

The basis for the Old Testament's demand of concern for the needy is clearly *religious*. The God of Israel was the defender of those who could not defend themselves, and the Israelites were to remember that they themselves were once in precisely that situation. When they implored Yahweh to hear their cries, "God heard their groaning . . . and knew their condition" (Ex. 2:24-25). Consequently, they had to demonstrate the same compassion toward the unfortunates in their society. Leviticus 19 makes the religious foundation for compassion even more explicit: "You shall be holy; for I the Lord your God am holy" (v. 2); and most of the specific injunctions of the chapter conclude with the statement, "I am the Lord [your God]" (v. 32 makes the connection especially clear: "You shall rise up before the hoary head, and honor the face of an old man, and you shall fear your God: I am the Lord"). On the prophetic side, Isaiah echoes this religious basis in the great poem of chapter 61 when Yahweh affirms, "For I the Lord love justice, I hate robbery and wrong; I will faithfully give them their recompense, and I will make an everlasting covenant with them" (v. 8).

Indeed, one can even discern a twofold manifestation of *"the image of God"* in this requirement to show concern for one's fellows, especially those who are less fortunate: First, as an earlier section of this chapter showed, human creation in the image of God means that human beings function as God's representatives on earth. Thus compassion for the poor and the defenseless is a way in which human beings serve in God's place and in God's name, doing that which God also does with regard to humanity, preeminently in the Exodus and again through the Servant. Second, inasmuch as all human beings appear to have been created in the "image of God," caring for them in some way becomes a way of demonstrating reverence and respect for God, that is, for the "reflection" of God in them.

The central importance of *community* also plays a role in the emphasis upon concern for the needy. As noted above, God lives with his human creatures in a community of compassion and faithful lovingkindness, and they therefore are to model their relations with their fellows upon this pattern. Furthermore, in Hebrew society, the individual (in the sense that the concept dominates contemporary thought) did not really exist; one existed only as part of the community.[15] To fail to provide for those who could not provide for themselves was tantamount to excluding them from the community. This failure in effect was equivalent to murder, just as to live out of relationship with Yahweh was "death." In short, the ancient Hebrews believed that Yahweh had created all persons in his own image and had called them into community with himself and through him with each other; thus they had to affirm an obligation to care for the less fortunate in their society just as God constantly showed his care for them through his mighty acts in their history.

Specific Concern for the Elderly

Attitudes and obligations toward the elderly can be seen as a special case, or a subset, of the more general concern for the disadvantaged in society. It is undeniable that the elderly throughout history have fit into this category; and the concern for the weak, the neglected, and the helpless that is generally characteristic of the Old Testament, Hebrew religion applied in particular to those whose ability to fend for themselves had been diminished by age. Supplemented by the recognition discussed above that the elderly occupy a special place in society because of their wisdom and experience, this point of view led throughout the Old Testament to numerous expressions of the obligations of the younger members of society toward their elders.

RESPECT   The most general obligation toward the elderly can be summarized as respect, which was due to all one's elders, whether related or not. Traditionally, Middle Eastern cultures have valued age highly, with honor and prestige increasing with years. The clearest statement in the Old Testament of this view is Leviticus 19:32, part of the key ethical chapter of the Holiness Code: "You shall rise up before the hoary head, and honor the face of an old man, and you shall fear your God: I am the Lord." Noteworthy here is the clear expression of the *religious* sanction for human moral behavior that is characteristic of Old Testament religion: Yahweh is interested in the treatment of the elderly, and their proper treatment is linked directly to the heart of Hebrew religion, namely, "fear of the Lord."

Jewish rabbinic tradition devotes considerable attention to the questions of who qualifies as having "a hoary head" and being "an old man," of whether age alone commands respect, and of how much "honor" should go to different categories of people (e.g., learned versus ignorant, Jew versus non-Jew).[16] Clearly, though, the command to "rise up before the hoary head, and honor the face of an old man"—regardless of later interpretation—must have originally been concerned simply with older people (however technically defined), and the intent certainly was to promote respect for them.

Several references testify to the importance of respecting the elderly by alluding to the results of the failure to do so. The disastrous outcome of Rehoboam's refusal to follow the advice of the older men among his advisers in favor of the harsh counsel of the younger (1 Kings 12:6ff.) has been noted already. In the story of Elisha and the forty-two boys mangled by the bears (2 Kings 2:23ff.), the boys' behavior qualifies as "ageism," representing as it does the reduction of the elderly to an object of scorn and ridicule based on a physical characteristic ("you baldhead"). Although Elisha's response to their taunting was hardly an example of the wisdom and forbearance that should come with age and experience, the narrator sounds a clear note of judgment upon the boys for their failure to show proper respect to an older man. The story perhaps suggests that respect is due the elderly whatever their personality. In short, the incident by its very outcome (horrific as it was) shows that in the text respect for the aged is a value of ultimate significance.

Furthermore, in a number of different places, lack of respect for the elderly or their mistreatment figures in Yahweh's displeasure or judgment. For example, in the psalm of lament with which Lamentations concludes, two of the factors demonstrating Judah's misery under Babylonian rule are that "no respect is shown to the elders" and "the old men have quit the city gate" (5:12, 14). Following Isaiah's description of "the day of the Lord," an oracle depicts the anarchy that calls forth God's judgment: One component is the clearly undesirable situation that "the youth will be insolent to the elder" (Is. 3:5). Later the prophet indicts Babylon because "on the aged you made your yoke exceedingly heavy" (Is. 47:6). Similarly, Deuteronomy warns the Israelites that "because you did not serve the Lord your God," Yahweh "will bring a nation against you from afar, . . . a nation of stern countenance, who shall not regard the person of the old or show favor to the young" (28:47, 49-50). If this criterion of a barbaric nation is one of the characteristics deemed worthy of mention by the historian, it not only demonstrates the centrality of respect for the elderly in Hebrew thought but also speaks forcefully to contemporary American society.

A similar point appears in a more positive vein in Zechariah 8:4, already cited as illustrating the contrast between the vitality of the young and the loss of mobility of the old: "Old men and old women shall again sit in the streets of Jerusalem, each with staff in hand for very age. And the streets of the city shall be full of boys and girls playing in its streets." Here the prophet depicts the restored Jerusalem, the city as he believes Yahweh intends it to be and in the midst of which God himself is dwelling. And one of the most significant characteristics of such a city—a city in which "they shall be my people and I shall be their God, in faithfulness and in righteousness" (8:8)—is the quality of life for "old men and old women" and "boys and girls," that is, the elderly and the children. Given this biblical vision of the urban life that the prophet claims God desires, one must ask of current treatment of these two groups, "How does our culture measure up?"—and shudder at the answer.

HONORING OF PARENTS   The respect for all older persons commanded by the Old Testament receives special emphasis in one particular instance, that of filial responsibility or the honor and the respect due one's parents (indeed, some commentators consider the general respect for one's elders to have its original roots in this more particular case). This is not surprising because, as Raphael Patai points out about the Middle East in general, "Of all the component features of Middle Eastern social organization the family is undoubtedly the most fundamental and most important."[17] And parents are of course the most fundamental and important component feature of the family, without whom no family would come into existence in the first place.

The clearest and most important statement of this obligation is found in the Decalogue, that set of fundamental rules governing the Hebrews' relationships with their God and with one another. The fifth commandment says, "Honor your father and your mother, that your days may be long in the land which the Lord your God gives you" (Ex. 20:12; cf. Deut. 5:16; Lev. 19:3). Books could be written on this commandment alone, and they have been.[18] Here only some of the most important points relevant to the basic concerns of this study can receive consideration.

Of great significance is the location of this commandment in the Decalogue, coming as it does in the pivotal spot between the first four commandments, which regulate human relationships with God, and the last five, which govern human interpersonal relationships. Thus the fifth commandment is the first one that is addressed to humans as social creatures, and therefore in some sense it states that responsibility to parents is fundamental to social morality. A strong stream of rabbinic interpretation has held that this commandment affirms that the earthly creators of life are reflections of the divine Creator (cf. the literal meaning of the now old-fashioned word "procreation": "to create for, on behalf of"). Thus one can understand the promise of Exodus 20:12, which is "determined on the principle of measure for measure: if you will honor the one who is the source of your life, you will be vouchsafed long life upon earth."[19]

But what does the commandment mean that is of practical value to this inquiry? Ronald E. Clements well states one crucial point on which virtually all commentators agree:

> The whole aim of this commandment is to secure positive support for ageing [sic] parents from their children, who are themselves assumed to be mature adults. When families lived together in large groups ageing parents who could no longer work were entirely dependent upon their children to support them economically. It is this care of the old that is demanded here.[20]

Indeed, as J. Edgar Park points out, family solidarity always ran so deep in Israel's life that this commandment would have seemed to a Hebrew *child* as superfluous as "thou shalt breathe" or "thou must eat." Thus he concludes that "it is directed to the adult citizen who is burdened with the care of an aged parent, and is a warning against the heathen habit of abandoning the aged when they can no longer support themselves."[21] The commandment certainly has something to say to young children also about obedience to their parents. This common interpretation, however, severely limits its applicability in a way that was not intended originally, and the application to adults as well needs to be brought to the attention of contemporary society. Rolf Knierim provides a fitting conclusion to this point (and a helpful transition to the next) when he says,

> It is generally assumed that the fifth commandment refers to an attitude of reverence and respect for parents, and such an attitude is certainly not excluded from its meaning. What is less well known, however, is that this commandment refers primarily to the material support of old parents by their adult children.[22]

This interpretation suggests another point that is central for the concerns of this study, namely, what "honor" means in the context of the fifth commandment. The preceding discussion has provided several clues already. The word "honor" in Hebrew comes from a root meaning "heavy" or "weighty"; to "honor" a parent, then, means to give weight to, to acknowledge the worth and the importance of that person. The use of this particular word (instead of, e.g., "obey") gave the commandment a much broader meaning. In fact, the parallel commandment in Leviticus 19:3 goes so far as to use the word "revere" ("fear"), which occurs elsewhere only with reference to God. Rabbinic tradition succinctly expressed what such an attitude involves:

83

> What is "fear" and what is "honour"? *"Fear"* means that he [the son] must neither stand in his [the father's] place nor sit in his place, nor contradict his words, nor tip the scales against him. *"Honour"* means that he must give him food and drink, clothe and cover him, lead him in and out.[23]

To honor one's parents, then, requires *more* than merely to treat them deferentially and to obey them when one is a child; there is a definite element of personal service involved, including not just attentiveness and obedience but the meeting of needs as well. Gerald Blidstein states that the Talmud affirms that "the honor of parents requires their support"; furthermore, it "implies that a son honors his parents by sharing his possessions with them, and suggests that he is required to do so." In fact, the "fundamental motif" of honor is "personal service": "To feed and clothe requires, primarily, not the financial expenditure for food and clothing, though it may imply that as well, but the physical deed itself."[24]

A look at several correlative "negative" commandments, all of which serve to heighten the already heavy requirement of proper consideration toward one's parents, will contribute to an understanding of the positive injunctions to "honor" and to "revere" parents. These verses in general prescribe the death penalty for children who dishonor their parents in various ways. Although this punishment stands in considerable disfavor today (and rabbinic tradition maintains that it never was carried out), its existence in the text indicates vividly the importance that Hebrew thought gave to the teaching contained in the fifth commandment. Exodus 21:15 states, "Whoever strikes his father or his mother shall be put to death," and verse 17 orders the same penalty for anyone who "curses" a parent (as does Lev. 20:9). Apparently, dishonoring in speech was as serious an offense as dishonoring in deed, not surprising given the power accorded to words in Hebrew thought and especially the real efficacy most ancient societies attributed to a curse. Deuteronomy 21:18-21 sets forth the procedure by which to punish an unrepentant disobedient son, namely, by stoning to death. And Deuteronomy 27:16 pronounces anyone who "dishonors" father or mother accursed. Several points about these passages are worthy of comment.

First, the Hebrew word for "curse" has a wider range of meaning than contemporary usage usually gives to the term: It connotes any action contrary to the respect and the honor due one's parents, tying it to its root meaning "to make light." Furthermore, the Code of Hammurabi specifies cutting off the offending hand as punishment for striking one's father.[25] The Torah, demonstrating even greater respect for one's parents, requires a more stringent penalty and includes mother as well as father. Finally, a comparison with Leviticus 24:16 shows that the punishment for cursing one's parent is exactly the same as that for cursing God, a parallel of great significance.

In fact, this point suggests another issue to consider in the examination of the meaning of the fifth commandment, namely, the fact that the Torah (and certainly the rabbinic interpretations of it) considers the honoring of father and mother to be a *mitzvah* as serious as the honoring of God. There can be no question of the place which *that* commandment held in Yahwism and later Judaism. The *Mekilta de-Rabbi Ishmael*, the rabbinic commentary on Exodus, states, "The honoring of one's father and mother is very dear in the sight of Him by whose word the world came into being. For He declared honoring them to be equal to honoring Him, fearing them equal to fearing Him, and cursing them equal to cursing Him."[26] It would be hard to think of a stronger way for a religion like Judaism to convey the importance of honoring one's parents than to equate such behavior with honoring the one true God.

This, then, is the basic meaning of the fifth commandment. Three related matters are of interest before moving on to examine some illustrations in the Hebrew Scriptures of the honoring of one's parents. Of particular significance is the fact that this commandment is the only one with a promise attached: "that your days may be long in the land which the Lord your God gives you" (Deut. 5:16 enhances the promise by adding, "and that it may go well with you"). The commandment that promises "length of days" as a reward for fulfilling it is thus also the one that requires a person to *honor father and mother*. An important though commonly unnoticed insight lies here: If one in fact does honor one's parents (in the ways discussed above), then their "long days" *will* be a blessing (recall the earlier discussion of the desirability of a long life in Hebrew thought precisely as a sign of God's favor). If one does not so honor them, however, then "length of days" becomes a curse rather than a blessing, a state of existence that indeed comes very close to the biblical Sheol, as a visit to most nursing homes today vividly demonstrates. And the curse is not only upon one's *parents* but upon *oneself* as well: As the child becomes old, that person too probably will fall prey to the very conditions of neglect and dishonor that his or her failure to honor parents has fostered.

Second, it should be noted that this commandment speaks only of responsibility to one's own *parents*, and it is probably going too far to extrapolate from this one law an obligation to care for the elderly in general (but support is strong for the view that such concern at least stems from filial responsibility, as, e.g., when Knierim says, "Society's protection of the elderly begins with protection by the family, basically expressed in the fifth commandment"[27]). At the very least, this commandment enjoins an apparently unshirkable obligation upon adult children to care for *their own* parents in their old age, an important message to contemporary Western society. Furthermore, given the Hebrew concern for the needy in general, as discussed above, as well as other specific provisions of the law (especially for widows, such as Ex. 22:22; Deut. 16:11; 27:19), it is not unreasonable to assume that Hebrew society neglected few old people (or, human nature being what it is, perhaps the most one can say is that few old people were *supposed* to be neglected!).

In this connection, Leviticus 19:32 deserves another brief look. As discussed earlier, rabbinic interpretations of Torah equate the honor due to parents and to God, but this particular verse seems to extend the equation to the elderly *in general:* "You shall rise up before the hoary head, and honor the face of an old man, and you shall fear your God: I am the Lord." The parallelism in language is obvious, with honor toward the elderly presented in the same breath, so to speak, as fear of God. And the formula, "I am the Lord," appears to give an explicit divine sanction to the threefold command that precedes. One must not give too much weight to a single verse, but Leviticus 19:32 provides at least some warrant for generalizing to all elderly the attitude of honor and respect that Torah commands toward parents.

A third and final point deserves mention. The attention given here to the fifth commandment does not intend to advocate a new legalism, as though all contemporary problems would be solved if everyone (or at least those who consider themselves Jews and Christians) would slavishly fulfill the letter of the law.[28] Considerable emphasis has been placed upon this injunction to honor parents not merely because it *is* one of the Ten Commandments but rather because Jews and Christians always have affirmed that *as* one of the Ten Commandments it is somehow fundamental to what God expects of his followers if they are to live in proper relationship with him and with each other.

Both the Old Testament and the New Testament depict a

God who does not want mere mechanical obedience to a certain set of rules; instead, God wants a certain kind of people, people who are properly related to him and therefore properly related to one another. And the community of believers always has maintained that the specific teachings of the Bible, especially those distilled in the Decalogue, show how people who are in a right relationship to God and to one another will act (or at least will want to act and will try to act). Clearly something more than slavish obedience to a law is required here. Indeed, this is recognized implicitly in the fact that the Decalogue itself is prefaced by a statement of Yahweh's redemption of Israel in the Exodus, linking obedience to the Law with remembrance of God's gracious and saving acts. As one would expect, then, fulfilling the Law has a religious foundation and motive, as *response* to the previously expressed grace of God.

FURTHER ILLUSTRATIONS IN THE OLD TESTAMENT   The rest of the Old Testament well illustrates the honoring of one's parents demanded in the laws (including provision for their needs in old age), thus lending support to the foregoing interpretation. Narrative demonstrates, Wisdom urges, and prophecy demands the respect for parents that was codified in the legal material.

Such respect and honor for parents first appears in the patriarchal narratives (perhaps even with Noah's sons Shem and Japheth, who "took a garment, laid it upon both their shoulders, and walked backward and covered the nakedness of their father" as he lay in a drunken stupor, Gen. 9:20ff.; Ham [father of Canaan?] failed to demonstrate similar respect and therefore suffered the curse to be a slave). In Genesis 45:9-13, Joseph commanded his brothers to "make haste and bring my father down here" to Egypt so that he might "provide for [him]" during the remaining years of the famine "lest [he] and [his] household, and all that [he has] come to poverty." Indeed, given that Joseph's first words to his brothers when he no longer could sustain his deception were, "I am Joseph; is my father still alive?" (45:3) it is hard to avoid the conclusion that his forgiveness of his treacherous siblings came largely from concern for his father (in fact, 50:15-17 suggests that they sensed this: Upon Jacob's death they sent a message to Joseph that their *father* had requested their pardon, concluding with their prayer that Joseph "forgive the transgression of the servants of the God *of your father*" [emphasis added]). Joseph further demonstrated his devotion to his aged father and his desire to honor him by his promise to bury him in Jacob's fathers' "burying place" (47:29-31) and by his fulfillment of the promise, although it entailed considerable effort (50:4-14). Moses later performed the same service for Joseph (Ex. 13:19).

The book of Ruth offers another concrete example of honor toward a parent (this time actually a widowed mother-*in-law*) that results in support and care. Ruth refused to leave Naomi and to return to her native Moab, preferring instead to go to Judah with her mother-in-law. There she gleaned for grain to feed the two of them, winning the favor of Boaz because, in his words, "All that you have done for your mother-in-law since the death of your husband has been fully told me. . . . The Lord recompense you for what you have done" (Ruth 2:11-12). After Boaz married Ruth, she bore a son, prompting Naomi's friends to exult:

> Blessed be the Lord, who has not left you this day without next of kin; and may his name be renowned in Israel! He shall be to you a restorer of life and a *nourisher of your old age;* for your daughter-in-law who loves you, who is more to you than seven sons, has borne him. (Ruth 4:14-15, emphasis added)

Clearly the assumption here is that the younger (even grandchildren) will care for the older, as Ruth had demonstrated. Incidentally, Naomi's exemplary behavior as the older person in the family deserves mention, especially early on when she refused to demand that her widowed daughters-in-law stay with her and provide for her.

The same requirement to honor and to care for aged parents illustrated in the stories just considered finds expression in the Wisdom literature as well, especially Proverbs. The book in fact begins with a reminder that the basic honor due one's parents is to learn from them the lessons conducive to successful living: "Hear, my son, your father's instruction, and reject not your mother's teaching; for they are a fair garland for your head, and pendants for your neck" (1:8-9). The most positive assertion specifically concerning care for older parents appears in 23:22, 24-25:

> Hearken to your father who begot you,
>   and do not despise your mother when she is old.
> The father of the righteous will greatly rejoice;
>   he who begets a wise son will be glad in him.
> Let your father and mother be glad,
>   let her who bore you rejoice.

A number of other sayings in Proverbs also illustrate the importance of children's attitudes toward their parents in determining the quality of the parents' lives: "A wise son makes a glad father, but a foolish son is a sorrow to his mother" (10:1; cf. 15:20); "A foolish son is a grief to his father and bitterness to her who bore him" (17:25; cf. v. 21; 19:13). Active disrespect comes in for even sharper condemnation: "If one curses his father or his mother, his lamp will be put out in utter darkness" (i.e., he will lose his life, 20:20; cf. the discussion of Ex. 21:17 above). Sufficient to bring down severe judgment is a mere hostile or sullen glance: "The eye that mocks a father and scorns to obey a mother will be picked out by the ravens of the valley and eaten by the vultures" (30:17; significantly, and better suited to the context, the Septuagint has "the old age of " for "to obey"). It comes as little surprise, then, that harsh criticism falls upon more aggressive assaults on the person or property of parents as well: "He who does violence to his father and chases away his mother is a son who causes shame and brings reproach" (19:26);[29] and "He who robs his father or his mother and says, 'That is no transgression,' is the companion of a man who destroys" (28:24). Finally, Proverbs 29:3 reverses the order, so to speak, and suggests as a *motive* for loving wisdom the result that comes from it—a happy parent: "He who loves wisdom makes his father glad."

The prophets echo the importance of concern for one's parents when, for example, Micah lamented the sorry state of affairs that had come upon Israel, a situation in which "the son treats the father with contempt, the daughter rises up against her mother, the daughter-in-law against her mother-in-law" (7:6; cf. Is. 3:5 for a similar but more general expression of woe: "And the people will oppress one another, every man his fellow and every man his neighbor; the youth will be insolent to the elder, and the base fellow to the honorable"). Ezekiel included among his oracles of indictment of Israel's "abominable deeds" the specific charge that "father and mother are treated with contempt in you" (22:7), and the prophet heard God complain that "the children rebelled against me" (20:21). Similarly, Yahweh, who had loved Israel as a parent loves a child, told Israel through Hosea that the nation deserved destruction because "the more I called them, the more they went from me" and "my people are bent on turning away from me" (11:2, 7). Note also Deuteronomy 32:6, which expresses Yahweh's disappointment in his people as that of a father whose children have failed to honor him: "Do you thus requite the Lord, you foolish and senseless people? Is not he your father, who created you, who made you and established you?" In the prophetic vision, failure to act with the proper honor and respect toward one's parents is both cause and effect of a disordered relationship with the very Center of life itself.

Summary

In conclusion, then, the Old Testament shows itself with regard to aging to be exactly what it is in every other regard, namely, a very *human* book. It implicitly or explicitly exhibits all the fears and the foibles, the strengths and the weaknesses, the successes and the failures that human beings know and observe concerning aging and old age. At the heart of all that the Old Testament has to say on this topic lie the twin anthropological affirmations, first encountered in the Genesis creation stories, that inform so much of Hebrew thought and life: First, human beings are created in "the image of God" and are therefore endowed with special power, place, role, and worth in the created order, and especially with the possibility of personal relationship with their Creator and with one another. And second, human beings are created to be in community, without which the individual, as contemporary society understands the term, hardly exists, and through which men and women are enabled (and required) to demonstrate their full humanity (and their likeness to God).

Regarding *aging itself,* the Old Testament recognizes the process of getting older as inevitable, as part of God's plan. Far from unduly resenting old age, however, the Old Testament sees "length of days" as a sign of righteousness, of blessing from God, and therefore as highly desirable. Indeed, the failure to experience old age, brought about by premature death, is precisely what does evoke anxiety. Frank recognition of the many losses associated with growing older—especially the decline of physical vitality—is nonetheless evident. The wisdom that is acquired through the accumulation of years and of consequent experience, however, can partially compensate for these losses.

Concerning *attitudes and obligations toward the elderly*, the Old Testament is quite clear. Running throughout is a strong concern for the weak, the disadvantaged, and the defenseless in general, and the aged in particular command this compassion. In addition, respect bordering on reverence is appropriate toward those who are older, especially one's own parents, toward whom one of the Ten Commandments requires honor as well. This honor, expected of adult as well as young children, includes not only obedience and deferential treatment but also material support, especially when the parents no longer are able to provide for themselves.

These various themes run deeply through the religion and the life of the Old Testament, and they gave to those who followed this religion a character and a commitment to family and community solidarity rarely seen in human history. As the attention of this study turns to the New Testament, a continuation of this central concern of the Old Testament will come as no surprise, given the fact that for the actors and the authors of the Christian Scriptures the Hebrew Bible was the basic source document of their faith.

NOTES

1. As is well known, the book of Genesis is composed of a number of different strata woven together by later editors into the form we know today. Chapters 1–3 contain two accounts of the creation of humanity: the first, 1:1–2:4*a*, from the Priestly source (P), and the second, 2:4*b*–3:24, from the Yahwist source (J). J is the oldest narrative source in the Hebrew Bible, written somewhere around 950 B.C.E.

P, although it contains older material, received its final redaction after the Exile (around 500 B.C.E.).

2. An important corollary of this affirmation follows: If human beings are in some fundamental yet derivative way "like God," they can know and understand *themselves* fully only as they come to know *God*, the One in whose very image and likeness they exist. Thus the crucial importance given in Hebrew religion to being in relationship with Yahweh (the only situation in which one could come to "know" God, especially given the existential understanding of knowledge expressed in Israel's thought) perhaps found a partial rationale in the concept of creation in God's image.

3. Lloyd Bailey, *Biblical Perspectives on Death* (Philadelphia: Fortress Press, 1979), p. 109. Ludwig Köhler (*Old Testament Theology*, trans. A. S. Todd [Philadelphia: Westminster Press, 1957], p. 148), after reviewing several attitudes toward death in the Old Testament, concludes that "it knows nothing of the idea that the death of man is punishment and a breach of God's original order" (italicized in the original).

4. Gerhard von Rad, *Genesis: A Commentary*, trans. John H. Marks, rev. ed. (Philadelphia: Westminster Press, 1972), p. 262.

5. Rolf Knierim, "Age and Aging in the Old Testament," in William M. Clements, ed., *Ministry with the Aging: Designs, Challenges, Foundations* (New York: Harper & Row, 1981), p. 22.

6. It should be noted, though, that despite the expression of loss of strength and ability to defend oneself in old age that runs throughout the psalm, an unconquerable sense of God's providence and faithfulness shines forth and is, in fact, the point of the whole effort: "Thou who hast made me see many sore troubles wilt revive me again; from the depths of the earth thou wilt bring me up again. . . . My lips will shout for joy, when I sing praises to thee; my soul also, which thou hast rescued" (Ps. 71:20, 23).

7. For all of Barzillai's self-deprecation, however, the fact that he achieved exactly what *he* wanted is significant and hardly a sign of weakness: He managed to maintain his own independence, even in the face of a royal request, without offending the king. Thus Barzillai provides an example of one who honestly recognized and faced the debilitations of old age yet who also exhibited both his own kind of strength and, perhaps most important, the wisdom to know how and when to exercise it.

8. Indeed, the entire book can be read as a reminder that those things that human beings tend to put stock in for personal fulfillment, including youth, beauty, and strength, *will* pass away as "vanity of vanities."

9. So Hans Walter Wolff (*Anthropology of the Old Testament*, trans. Margaret Kohl [Philadelphia: Fortress Press, 1974], p. 125) renders *yeladim* (vv. 8, 10, 14), which the RSV translates simply as "young men." In his discussion of Wisdom in ancient Israel, John L. McKenzie (*A Theology of the Old Testament* [Garden City, N.Y.: Doubleday Image Books, 1976], p. 214) says, "Wisdom begins with listening to one's elders; the wise men take a dim view of the new and experimental in living. . . . In the normal course of events, the wise man goes with experience; the assumption is not that the elders always know best, but that one cannot make a wise decision in a new situation or even recognize that it is a new situation unless one has mastered the wisdom of collective experience."

10. Benjamin Blech, "Judaism and Gerontology," in Carol LeFevre and Perry LeFevre, eds., *Aging and the Human Spirit: A Reader in Religion and Gerontology* (Chicago: Exploration Press, 1981), p. 14. Edmund Byrne ("Death and Aging in Technopolis," in Patrick L. McKee, ed., *Philosophical Foundations of Gerontology* [New York: Human Sciences Press, 1982], p. 70) makes the case even more pointedly: "But if the day ever comes when our hunger for community is intense enough to make us ask basic questions about where we are really going . . . , we may then remember

what simple folk have never forgotten: if one must go where one has never been, it can do no harm to ask directions of another who is already there."

11. Yahweh's response is significant: "Do not say, 'I am only a youth'; for to all to whom I send you you shall go, and whatever I command you you shall speak. Be not afraid of them, for I am with you to deliver you, says the Lord" (Jer. 1:7-8). Despite the usual correlation of wisdom with age, *God* remains sovereign and can use any vehicle he wishes to fulfill his purposes.

12. G. Henton Davies, "Elder in the OT," in George A. Buttrick et al., eds., *The Interpreter's Dictionary of the Bible*, vol. E–J (Nashville: Abingdon Press, 1962), p. 72.

13. S. H. Blank, "Age, Old," in Buttrick, *Interpreter's Dictionary*, vol. A–D, p. 55. Still, Blank concludes that "indeed the experience and wisdom of the older man would fit him for such judicial and administrative responsibilities as the elder discharged."

14. Theodor Vriezen, *An Outline of Old Testament Theology*, trans. S. Neuijen (Newton, Mass.: Charles T. Branford, 1970), p. 388. Cf. Wolff, *Anthropology*, pp. 186-91 and 214-22, for further information on this important concept.

15. The much discussed notion of "corporate personality" in ancient Israel provides helpful information on this point. As H. Wheeler Robinson (*Corporate Personality in Ancient Israel* [Philadelphia: Fortress Press, 1964], p. 26) points out, the Hebrew's participation in the corporate personality of the society was especially important because Yahweh's "covenant was with the nation, not with the individual Israelites except as members or representatives of the nation."

16. A helpful summary can be found in Shelomoh Yosef Zevin, "By the Light of Halakhah," in Norman Lamm, ed., *The Good Society: Jewish Ethics in Action* (New York: Viking Press, 1974), pp. 120-31. See also Gerald Blidstein, *Honor Thy Father and Mother* (New York: KTAV Publishing House, 1975), passim.

17. Raphael Patai, *Society, Culture, and Change in the Middle East*, 3d ed., enlarged (Philadelphia: University of Pennsylvania Press, 1969), p. 84.

18. See especially the thorough treatment of the development of interpretation of this verse within Judaism by Blidstein, *Honor Thy Father.*

19. Umberto Cassuto, *A Commentary on the Book of Exodus*, trans. Israel Abrahams (Jerusalem: Magnes Press, 1967), p. 246. For a discussion of the rabbinic interpretations, see Blidstein, *Honor Thy Father*, pp. 1-8.

20. Ronald E. Clements, *Exodus*, The Cambridge Bible Commentary of the New English Bible (London: Cambridge University Press, 1972), p. 125.

21. J. Edgar Park, "Exodus: Exposition," in George A. Buttrick et al., eds., *The Interpreter's Bible*, vol. 1 (Nashville: Abingdon Press, 1952), p. 985. Cf. Brevard Childs, *The Book of Exodus: A Critical, Theological Commentary* (Philadelphia: Westminster Press, 1974), p. 418: "Lying at the heart of the original prohibition was a command which protected parents from being driven out of the home or abused after they could no longer work"; J. Coert Rylaarsdam, "Exodus: Exegesis," in Buttrick, *Interpreter's Bible*, vol. 1, p. 985: "This commandment most especially refers to the treatment of helpless aged dependents"; Wolff, *Anthropology*, p. 183: "It is not only young people who are addressed, but grown-up children particularly, who live together in the family group together with their parents, who are now getting to the stage of needing help."

22. Knierim, "Age and Aging in the Old Testament," in Clements, *Ministry with the Aging*, p. 29. He cites Gen. 45:9-11 for support, where Joseph sends his brothers to fetch his elderly father Jacob with the message, "I will provide for you."

23. *Kiddushin* 31b, *The Babylonian Talmud*, Seder Nashim, vol. 4, ed. Isidore Epstein, trans. H. Freedman (London: Soncino Press, 1936), pp. 154-55. Blidstein (*Honor Thy Father*, p. 43) points out that when fulfilling the commandment to honor a

parent would bring about great loss to the child, and failing to do so would cause slight annoyance or inconvenience to the parent, "the guideline is obvious: when such a conflict arises, the effect on the parent becomes an absolute, without respect to the effect on the son." It is worthy of note that the Mishnah (*Kiddushin* 1:7, in *The Mishnah*, trans. Herbert Danby [Oxford: Oxford University Press, 1933], p. 322) applies such *mitzvot* to both sons and daughters: "All obligations of a son towards his father enjoined in the Law are incumbent both on men and on women."

24. Blidstein, *Honor Thy Father*, pp. 60, 61, 47. Later, Blidstein concludes that, based on this commandment to "honor" one's parents, a "concrete social ethic" in which "children were made responsible for the economic security of their parents" was hammered out by Judaism (p. 73).

25. "The Code of Hammurabi," 195, in *Ancient Near East Texts Relating to the Old Testament*, ed. James B. Pritchard, 3d ed. (Princeton: Princeton University Press, 1969), p. 175.

26. Bahodesh 8, in *Mekilta de-Rabbi Ishmael*, ed. and trans. Jacob Z. Lauterbach, vol. 2 (Philadelphia: Jewish Publication Society of America, 1933), pp. 257-58. Cf. *Kiddushin* 30b-31a, *Babylonian Talmud*, p. 149: "Our Rabbis taught: There are three partners in man: the Holy One, blessed be He, the father, and the mother. When a man honors his father and his mother, the Holy One says, 'I consider that as meritorious as if I had lived with them and he had honored Me.' "

27. Knierim, "Age and Aging in the Old Testament," in Clements, *Ministry with the Aging*, p. 28. Wolff (*Anthropology*, p. 123) comments, "Behind the commandment concerning parents in the Decalogue, we can descry real problems about the care of the old."

28. Brevard Childs (*Book of Exodus*, p. 439) asserts that "the theological challenge for the church today is to give to the divine commandments a form of 'flesh and blood' which not only strives to be obedient to God in the hearing of his word, but is equally serious in addressing its imperatives with boldness to the contemporary world." Part of this task is to "reinterpret with new power the imperative to love one another before the threat of technological dehumanization." This book is an attempt to respond to the challenge of which Childs speaks.

29. Wolff (*Anthropology*, p. 183) sees this proverb as speaking "against the wish to inherit prematurely." Charles T. Frisch ("Proverbs: Exegesis," in Buttrick, *Interpreter's Bible*, vol. 4, p. 895) comments, "A son whose aged parents are dependent upon him is described here."

AGING AND THE
ELDERLY IN THE
NEW TESTAMENT

CHAPTER THREE

Although the Old Testament may not address the issues of aging in exactly the categories that would most facilitate examination of the subject, the preceding chapter has shown that the Hebrew Scriptures say a great deal that is of significance about both aging and obligations toward the elderly. As this inquiry turns now to the New Testament, even less material of a direct, explicit nature appears. Still, the Christian Scriptures contain considerable information that can provide guidance in responding to the problems of today.

The Authority of the Sources

At the outset, a word must be said about an important matter. Christians historically have looked to Jesus of Nazareth as the model for appropriate attitudes and behavior. Modern biblical scholarship, however, has shown that deriving guidelines for Christian thought and action from the life and the teaching of Jesus is no longer the simple matter that it once may have been thought to be, because one cannot know for sure exactly what the life of Jesus actually *was*. Furthermore, the apocalyptic framework of first-century Christianity renders impossible simply taking the statements attributed to Jesus and applying them to the twentieth century.

Even on the most skeptical reading, however, the records of Jesus in the Gospels do express the canonical conclusions of the early church and are therefore in a significant way central to contemporary Christian thinking, even if one grants that they might reflect not only the mind of Jesus but also the views and interests of the evangelists and the factions they represented. Whatever its absolute historicity, one can find depicted in the Gospel portrait of Jesus, at the very least, certain themes that were normative for the Christian community's self-understanding. Among these are the centrality of the kingdom of God and its demand for righteousness (in terms of both personal integrity and social justice), the incarnation of divine compassion, and the necessity for self-sacrifice when the needs of self and neighbor conflict. With Dodd, Jeremias, and Keck, then, this study will take a more conservative approach to the question of the relevance of the biblical portraits of Jesus for contemporary Christian ethical reflection. This approach acknowledges that much of the New Testament material reflects the thinking of the early church, but it also recognizes that that thinking plays the role of arbiter of subsequent Christian thought.

Having said this, however, one still confronts problems. First, as with several other topics of interest today, the Gospels do not record any teachings of Jesus that explicitly and directly address aging and the elderly. Nevertheless, one can discern with some confidence what the Gospel writers believed Jesus to have taught—and, of at least equal importance, to have practiced—with regard to aging. Second, the quest to discover Jesus' view of aging encounters another serious obstacle: The subject of the inquiry did not himself die "in a good old age, an old man and full of years," a fact that has deprived subsequent investigators of evidence about how he would have handled aging and old age. Any interpreter who is also a disciple, though, and aware of what the human race would have lost if Jesus had not died when and as he did, accepts the paucity of records available concerning Jesus' attitude and teaching on this subject and sets about making the best of what there is to work with.

New Testament Attitudes Toward Aging

The Incarnation and the Image of God

Emil Brunner has called the Incarnation "the funda-mental Christian truth," and Christianity as the world has known it for twenty centuries is difficult to imagine without this central doctrine. One can argue that everything else could go, but if this tenet remained, the basic faith would be intact; if, on the other hand, the truth of the "Word made flesh" no longer were accepted, all other Christian doctrines would be emptied of their theological and religious impact.

Chapter 2 pointed out that the concept of human creation in the image of God is central to Old Testament anthropology; likewise, the doctrine of the Incarnation is essential to the Christian view of human nature. In fact, the two ideas serve analogous functions in the religions of the Old and New Testaments. That is, the creation of human beings in God's image meant for Israel that every person possessed worth and dignity and deserved to be treated accordingly. Similarly, for Christianity the clearest confirmation of the value and the significance of every human being comes from the Incarnation, from the fact that God took human form: "In the beginning [note the echo of Gen. 1] was the Word, and the Word was with God, and the Word was God. . . . And the Word became flesh and dwelt among us" (Jn. 1:1, 14). The Incarnation shows unequivocally that human nature is worthy of the most intimate union possible with divine nature. The doctrine thus affirms the truth contained in the Old Testament notion of human creation in the image of God and underscored in the statement of Genesis 1:31 upon the completion of creation: "And God saw everything that he made, and behold, it was very good."

This affirmation suggests another important implication of the doctrine of the Incarnation, one that is also akin to an aspect of the image of God discussed in chapter 2. Supplementing the message of Genesis 1, the Incarnation allows Christians to affirm strongly the goodness of the created order, including the human body. Thus concern about the welfare of the body is totally legitimate (though not ultimate) in Christian thought because the body *is* valuable. If it were not, then its decay would be of no moment and no cause for anxiety and despair (cf. the Greek notion of the body as a prison for the soul, to be escaped if possible). But Christianity asserts that God's assumption of a human body in the Incarnation imparted a high value to all embodiment. Thus the almost universal human experience of concern about the waning of bodily powers as one grows old reflects a theological truth: The body *is* important and its deterioration can be legitimately lamented. Of course, Christianity is equally strong in affirming, contrary to modern materialism, that the body's value is not ultimate.

These two key anthropological affirmations, human creation in the image of God and the Incarnation, can be put together in the following manner, of considerable relevance to this inquiry: If human beings are created in the image of God and thus possess a "likeness" to the divine nature shared by no other creatures, then the only way for them to be true to themselves is to do as God does, in short, to live in accord with their own real nature. Christians assert that in the Incarnation, humans have the clearest example of how God would live (indeed, *did* live) as a human being and therefore of how they must strive to live if they are to fulfill their nature. Thus the greatest freedom—the freedom truly to be *oneself,* to live as one ought to live—comes precisely when one submits one's own will to the will of God, submerges one's *self*-interest, and perhaps even gives up oneself for the sake of God and others. Only in this way does one realize one's creation in the image and likeness of God by reflecting God's action in one's own deeds (cf. Phil. 2:5-8; Mk. 14:36; 8:34-37; 2 Cor. 3:17*b*).

As with the Old Testament doctrine of creation in God's image, then, the New Testament doctrine of the Incarnation has many implications for Christian attitudes toward aging, especially given the central role that a person's attitude toward the body plays in one's reaction to growing older.

Attitudes Toward the Body and Aging

Indeed, the place to start in this study of attitudes toward aging in the New Testament is with a consideration of the major source of ideas about the body, namely, the writings of Paul.[1] Examination of his writings will provide considerable information about what the New Testament can contribute to a contemporary view of aging.

Paul uses two words that are important for this discussion: *sarx,* usually translated "flesh," and *soma,* generally rendered as "body." Popular misconceptions abound concerning the meanings of the two terms, and scholars differ as to Paul's exact understanding and use of

101

the words. In general, though, John A. T. Robinson's distinctions, presented in *The Body: A Study in Pauline Theology*, are accepted. *Sarx* refers basically to "the flesh-substance common to men and beasts," but its meaning is not limited to the material from which a *soma* is made or merely to a particular part of the body in contrast to the whole. Instead, for Paul *sarx* "is the whole body, or, better, the whole person, considered from the point of view of his external, physical existence" (pp. 17-18). Furthermore, *sarx* describes the human being as *human*, that is, as distinct from God: "Flesh represents mere man, man in contrast with God—hence man in his weakness and mortality" (p. 19). As such, *sarx* is subject to two constant characteristics: infirmity and mortality (p. 20). Perhaps the most significant aspect of Paul's understanding of *sarx* for this study is expressed by Robinson when he says (acknowledging Bultmann), " 'The mind of the flesh' stands primarily for a denial of man's dependence on God and for a trust in what is of human effort or origin" (p. 25). In short, for Paul *sarx* refers to human existence as embodied beings who deny their absolute dependence on their Creator and try to "go it alone" in pursuit of their own desires and ends.

Soma differs significantly from *sarx*: "While [*sarx*] stands for man, in the solidarity of creation, in his distance from God, [*soma*] stands for man, in the solidarity of creation, as made for God."[2] That is, *sarx* describes the person precisely in that "earth-ward" aspect of human existence that prevents the fellowship with God intended in the creation; *soma* expresses human existence in its "God-ward" aspect that is capable of enjoying restored communion with its Creator (cf. 1 Cor. 6:19-20: "Do you not know that your body [*soma*] is a temple of the Holy Spirit within you, which you have from God? . . . So glorify God in your body," where the *soma* is both the location and the medium for serving and praising God). This distinction between the *soma*'s capacity for relationship with God and the *sarx*'s lack of such capacity explains why Paul can assert that the *soma* and not the *sarx* will inherit the kingdom of God and share in the Resurrection of Christ (1 Cor. 15:50, 53).

When the Christian ceases to live "according to the flesh," earthly, physical concerns and relationships do not stop or become unimportant. They simply no longer are determined by one's own will but rather by God's purposes for one's life; and one's body (i.e., one's *soma*) can become what it really is: the vehicle through which God's Spirit can lead one to the destiny for which one was created. Accordingly, asceticism is not a necessary result of ceasing to be "in the flesh" and coming to live "in the Spirit"; rather, a healthy concern about one's physical body (now serving its *proper* function) is perfectly appropriate.

Robinson moves more toward the topic of this study when he says, "For to live 'after the flesh,' on the assumption, namely, that man's life consists simply in the [*sarx*], in his self-sufficiency apart from God, is *ipso facto* to accept the end of the [*sarx*] as the end of man, that is, dissolution and death" (p. 34). As Paul himself bluntly put it, "To set the mind on the flesh is death . . . for if you live according to the flesh you will die" (Rom. 8:6, 13). Paul's terminology and meaning thus may be applied to the issue of contemporary attitudes toward aging as follows: Today's emphasis on youth, beauty, strength, and agility (not to mention wealth, material possessions, and other such external determinants of personal value), with the consequent denigration of everyone who does not exhibit such characteristics, is certainly an indisputable exhibition of what Paul meant by living "according to the flesh." Ordering one's life by these "worldly standards" is far from what God desires for his human creatures, and such behavior prevents one from moving away from "fleshly" (i.e., *self*-directed) life toward "somatic" (i.e., *God*-directed) life.[3]

Genuine concern for the *soma*, however, almost invariably leads to what *sarx* perceives as damage to itself. Examples might be the pain of dieting to lose weight, the discomfort of aerobic exercise to promote one's overall well-being, or the agonizing prospect of disfiguring surgery to remove a life-threatening tumor. The important point is that *genuine* concern for the body may involve pain and even "damage" to the flesh. In Paul's view, the ascendancy of the *soma* must lead ultimately to the destruction and the loss of the *sarx* (cf. 1 Cor. 15:36, 42-45, 50-57).

The problem arises when damage is done to the *soma* for the sake of the *sarx*. Concern for the *sarx*—as, for example, in the extremes to which many people go to deny their aging, or in judgments of the worth of others on the basis of external characteristics like youth and appearance—must not blind one to the *soma*'s demands, nor can deterioration of the *sarx* lead one to fail to discern the *soma* or to grant its enduring (and ultimate) value.

In sum, *sarx* in Pauline thought refers to human existence as embodied beings who deny their absolute dependence on their Creator, thus assuring for themselves a life of disorder and dissatisfaction because of their alienation from the only One who can give them what they are seeking so desperately on their own. As such, the "flesh" must deteriorate and be a source of pain, frustration, and disappointment, especially because one living "after the flesh" fails to cultivate the *soma* and to acknowledge its centrality in a properly ordered life. Only in accepting dependence upon God can the "body" (*soma*) become a vehicle of hope and joy and the decline of the flesh be accepted as a necessary aspect of the things that are seen and transient, which must pass away if one is to attain the things that are unseen and eternal.

"Do Not Be Anxious About Your Life"

Although the Gospels do not record any direct teachings of Jesus concerning aging itself, they do report several statements and incidents that give some indication of the attitude toward aging held by both Jesus and the society in which he lived. In fact, the concept of body just discussed can help one to understand a particularly fruitful passage in the Sermon on the Mount (Mt. 6:25-34; cf. Lk. 12:22-31).[4] Jesus went to some lengths to urge his hearers not to "be anxious about your life" (Mt. 6:25)—sound enough general advice, especially in today's anxiety-laden world but the passage conveys a more specific message. In order to make his point concerning the foolishness of excessive worry about the necessities of life, Jesus used the illustration of birds and flowers, which do not "sow or reap or gather into barns or toil or spin"; yet God provides bountifully for them. God's provision for their welfare is thus not dependent at all upon their productivity or usefulness, a fact with obvious relevance to any discussion of aging and the elderly. Jesus asserted, then, "If your heavenly Father provides for them [despite their non-productivity], how much more does he care for you?" Although one cannot build a "theology of aging" on this point alone, it is worthy of note that Jesus—consistent with what he is portrayed elsewhere as teaching, and in a passage that explicitly mentions length of life—did not make God's care for human beings at all dependent upon what they contribute to society.

In addition, the passage offers another worthwhile warning for people today who are overly concerned about growing older (along with any number of other things). In a statement that indicates his keen insight into human nature (and that is echoed today in much medical advice about stress reduction), Jesus asked, "And which of you by being anxious can add one cubit to his span of life?" (Mt. 6:27; cf. Ps. 39:5) This question of course does not imply that Jesus considered concern about length of life illegitimate, but it does express the truth that one of the surest ways *not* to achieve the desired goal is to be *unduly* concerned about it! Indeed, the principle expressed in Jesus' key teaching of losing one's life by trying to save it underlies a great deal of his message.

The Role of Older People

The second half of this chapter will discuss the early church's view of its obligations *toward* older people, especially widows; a brief look here at *their* responsibilities and activities will contribute significantly to an appreciation of the New Testament's attitude toward aging and the aged.

Luke presents several older people in a quite favorable light in chapters 1 and 2. Zechariah and Elizabeth, the parents of John the Baptist, are described as "advanced in years" (1:7; cf. vv. 18, 36). Nonetheless, Zechariah was still "serving as priest before God" (1:8), and he even had the honor of entering the temple to burn incense at the altar. Obviously his age did not disqualify him from these important duties. Furthermore, a striking parallel exists between this story and that of the pregnancy of Sarah when she and Abraham were "old, advanced in age" (Gen. 18). Here again the message is certainly, in part at least, that God can use any vehicle to accomplish his purposes, even one that may seem to be past its usefulness: "For with God nothing will be impossible" (Lk. 1:37; cf. Gen. 18:14). The story, however, also contains an implicit warning to the elderly not to let their age become an excuse for doubting God's concern for them: The angel told Zechariah that he would be struck dumb for the duration of Elizabeth's pregnancy "because you did not believe my words, which will be fulfilled in their time" (Lk. 1:20).

In Luke 2, two more older people appear in a positive

106

light. The wording of verses 26 and 29 suggests that Simeon was an old man whom God had allowed to live until he should see the Messiah, perhaps because Simeon was "righteous and devout," filled with the Holy Spirit (v. 25). Age of course may not have been the only reason for Simeon's religious insight, but the fact remains that the response of an older man is what Luke chose to mention explicitly here. The perspicacity demonstrated by the aged Simeon was exhibited also by the prophetess Anna, about whose "great age" Luke leaves no doubt (2:36-38). Her advanced age, however, did not deter her from a day-and-night vigil of fasting and prayer in the temple, and she immediately recognized Jesus as the awaited "redemption of Israel." Although such insight and harmony with the divine are not limited to the elderly, it is noteworthy that, apart from the parents of Jesus, the only persons mentioned by Luke in these chapters as having a role in the advent of the Messiah are old.

On the role of widows in particular, the Pastoral Epistles (especially 1 Tim. 5:3-16) are the best sources for information. Widows over sixty (certainly elderly in that day) were to be "enrolled" if they met certain qualifications, thereby assuming somewhat of an "official" status within the Christian community. The standards were not low: To be enrolled the widow must have "been the wife of one husband; and she must be well attested for her good deeds, as one who has brought up children, shown hospitality, washed the feet of the saints, relieved the afflicted, and devoted herself to doing good in every way" (vv. 9-10).

The letter to Titus provides another expression of what was expected of the elderly: "Bid the older women likewise to be reverent in behavior . . . ; they are to teach what is good, and so train the young women to love their husbands and children, to be sensible, chaste, domestic, kind, and submissive to their husbands, that the word of God may not be discredited" (2:3-5). Older women thus had important work to do in preparing subsequent generations for their proper place in the Christian family and the church. Second Timothy 1:5 provides a concrete example of the fulfillment of this responsibility: The author of the letter presents an "older woman," Timothy's grandmother Lois, as a model of the "sincere faith" that also dwelt in his mother Eunice and ultimately in Timothy himself (cf. 3:15). Surely Lois had been reverent and had trained her daughter (and even grandson) well.

Of course, not all elderly people lived up to these high expectations and ideals. For example, the passage from Titus cited above to illustrate the weighty responsibilities of older women contains a warning "not to be slanderers or slaves to drink," which the author obviously thought was needed. Verse 2 similarly urges that "the older men be temperate, serious, sensible, sound in faith, in love, and in steadfastness." These statements affirm that old age as well as youth can be a time of particular temptations, which one must recognize and resist. A little later, Chrysostom, writing between 375 and 386 C.E., did not present a very positive view of widows on the relief rolls of the church: "For widows are a class who, both on account of their poverty, their age and natural disposition, indulge in unlimited freedom of speech (so I had best call it); and they make an unseasonable clamor and idle complaints and lamentations about matters for which they ought to be grateful."[5]

Two more verses shed further light on this matter. The author of 1 Timothy, writing words of advice to a young minister, apparently was aware that many older people have the unpleasant tendency not to credit youth with its full due; so he urged his protégé, "Let no one despise your youth, but set the believers an example in speech and conduct, in love, in faith, in purity" (4:12). This admonition makes clear that those who are older have a responsibility not to judge someone on the basis of age alone, and furthermore to accept the fact that youth sometimes can show age the way.

On the other hand, in 2 Timothy 2:22, the author acknowledges that in youth feelings run high and need to be moderated with more mature qualities: "So shun youthful passions and aim at righteousness, faith, love, and peace." The message in this passage seems to be that no age group has a monopoly on either good or bad characteristics, and that each has responsibilities toward the other.

Elders

A brief consideration of the New Testament usage of the term "elder" (*presbuteros*) leads to a similar conclusion. Obviously modeled on the Jewish institution, the elders of the early Christian church occupied the same position at the center of religious life. The Pastoral Epistles provide information about qualifications for the office and its responsibilities (especially Tit. 1:5-7; 1 Tim. 5:17-22; cf. Jas. 5:14; 1 Pet. 5:1-5) but fail to answer an important question: How old were the elders? The scholarly consensus is not surprising: Considering all the evidence, the term "elder" cannot be seen as only a designation of age.

Thus the conclusion reached concerning elders in the Old Testament is appropriate here as well: Authority in the early church was not necessarily a function of age alone (cf. Timothy, e.g.). The fact that the leaders bore the title "elder," however, suggests that the Old Testament correlation of age with wisdom and fitness for authority continued into Christianity, though not in any more absolute way than in the Hebrew Scriptures. That the early church exhibited such implicit (and often explicit) honor and respect for its older members is not surprising given that the first Christians were Jews and that the Jerusalem church exerted considerable influence upon the early missionary effort.

The Final Consummation

One further pastoral word to those who are troubled by the prospect of growing older appears in Revelation 21. In language reminiscent of Isaiah 65, John of Patmos relates his magnificent vision of "a new heaven and a new earth" (v. 1). Significantly, and in keeping with Jewish apocalyptic in general, the language suggests not the destruction of the current created order and some kind of ethereal existence "in heaven"; rather, the implication is that God will cleanse, purify, and renew the creation and thus will provide in effect a restored Eden for the saints to inhabit. God himself will dwell with the faithful in the new Jerusalem (vv. 2-3), as he had intended from the beginning. Verse 4 contains the ultimate word that the New Testament (and Christianity) have to offer with regard to life, death, and the process that leads from one to the other, namely, aging: God "will wipe away every tear from their eyes, and death shall be no more, neither shall there be mourning nor crying nor pain any more, for the former things have passed away." When God is ready, the seer affirms, he will bring an end to death and thus to the pain and the tears of parting. In this way he will overcome the real problem of growing older—having to say good-bye to all that one holds dear, including not only friends and loved ones but also one's own self as the body deteriorates. Ultimately, the One who is himself "the beginning and the end" will satisfy all human thirsts with water, not from the legendary "fountain of youth," but from the very "fountain of the water of life" itself (v. 6).

A final comment: Verse 5 states, "And he who sat upon the throne said, 'Behold, I make all things new' " (cf. Is. 65:17). The affirmation refers primarily to the ultimate renewing that will occur in the *eschaton*, but the use of the present tense suggests that renewal does not have to await "the close of the age." Indeed, the New Testament depicts

God as constantly making things new in the here and now (e.g., 2 Cor. 3:18; 4:16-18; 5:16-17; Col. 3:1-4), a fact that can be of considerable comfort to those who are discouraged about becoming old.

A concrete example of this point can be found in an incident from John's Gospel that sheds further light on the New Testament's attitude toward aging and the elderly.[6] In a well-known story, Nicodemus responded to Jesus' statement about the need to be "born anew," "How can a man be born when he is old?" (3:4) The Greek word *geron* certainly means advanced in years, leading to the conclusion that Nicodemus himself was an old man, a conclusion further supported by his being called "a ruler of the Jews." Thus the Jesus of John's Gospel did not consider even an old man incapable of a truly life-changing act, one as significant as being "born anew." This fact should give pause to those who want to dismiss the elderly as "too set in their ways" to change themselves or to embrace anything new.

Obligations Toward the Elderly

In addition to providing valuable information about the appropriate attitude toward one's own aging, the New Testament says quite a bit about responsibilities and obligations toward those who are older. As with the Old Testament, this concern finds expression both generally and specifically.

Love for Others

The most general principle governing obligations toward others lies at the very heart of the Christian gospel. Central to the teaching of Jesus—indeed, embodied in his life—was the Great Commandment (Mt. 22:34-40) enjoining love of God and love of neighbor as the fulfillment of the Law (and, significantly, showing the clearly *religious* roots of Jesus' ethical teaching). John depicts Jesus in his farewell remarks to his disciples as asserting that to abide in his love they must obey his commandments. Jesus then says, "This is my commandment, that you love one another as I have loved you" (Jn. 15:12).

As later canonical writers strove to work out the meaning of the life, death, and Resurrection of Jesus, they naturally put this major theme of his teaching and action at the center. Paul, following the lead of his Lord, throughout his writings so emphasizes the command to love that in Galatians 6:2 he even calls love (understood, significantly, as "bearing one another's burdens") "the law of Christ" (cf. Gal. 5:14—"For the whole law is fulfilled in one word, 'You shall love your neighbor as yourself' "; also Rom. 13:10— "therefore love is the fulfilling of the law"). Nowhere is Paul's understanding of love more clearly articulated (or the Christian ideal more beautifully expressed) than in 1 Corinthians 13, Paul's great hymn to love.

The love that Paul describes in 1 Corinthians 13 is clearly that expected of all Christians (Mt. 25:31-46; Jn. 15:12-17; 1 Jn. 4:7-21). As Wolfgang Schrage puts it, "Love means being free from oneself and being available to others, and this is the quintessence and center of all [Paul's] individual demands (Rom. 13:8-10; Gal. 5:14)."[7] Although no one attains the ideal, that failure does not relieve the Christian from trying to live up to it, as far as is humanly possible. The goal is certainly not to be rejected simply because it is unattainable (any more than the "impossibility" of fulfilling the demands of Jesus in the Sermon on the Mount means that they have no relevance to the moral lives of Christians).

Other New Testament epistles express the centrality and the necessity of Christian love clearly and forcefully. James 2:1-13, for example, reflects some of the themes of Paul's thought concerning love, mutuality, and community among

Christians. First John 4:11 states, "Beloved, if God so loved us, we also ought to love one another," and verses 19-20 continue: "We love, because he first loved us. If any one says, 'I love God,' and hates his brother, he is a liar" (cf. 2 Jn. 6). What does "John" mean by love? Not superficial emotion, not professions of concern and sympathy, but something much more concrete: "By this we know love, that he laid down his life for us; and we ought to lay down our lives for the brethren" (1 Jn. 3:16).

Of course, not many Christians today are called upon to sacrifice their lives for others, and the author of 1 John must have anticipated that because he immediately added, "But if any one has the world's goods and sees his brother [which one can certainly read as 'his or her mother' or 'father' or 'any older person'] in need, yet closes his heart against him, how does God's love abide in him? Little children, let us not love in word or speech but in deed and truth" (1 Jn. 3:17-18). Here is yet another expression of the unity of religious faith and ethical expression that this study has shown to be an integral and indispensable component of biblical religion (cf. 1 Jn. 2:4-6, which concludes, "he who says he abides in [Jesus Christ] ought to walk in the same way in which he walked").

The Command to Be a Servant

That the later canonical interpreters of Jesus' life and teaching should stress the centrality of love that reaches out to others is not surprising, given Jesus' demand, based upon his own example, that anyone who would follow him must be a servant of others. In Mark 10:43-45, for instance, Jesus said to his disciples (after James and John had tried to gain a position of favor), "Whoever would be great among you must be your servant, and whoever would be first among you must be slave of all. For the Son of man also came not to be served but to serve, and to give his life as a ransom for many" (cf. Mk. 9:35 and parallels).

The Lukan parallel to this story (22:24-27) contains an interesting bit of information. Jesus' response to his disciples includes the comment, "rather let the greatest among you become as the youngest" (v. 26). The obvious implication is that in Jesus' mind there was a correlation between "greatness" (i.e., preeminence, authority, prestige) and age. Otherwise, why would the demand that the "greatest" become as the "youngest" be analogous in his teaching to the demand that the master become as the slave and the leader as one who serves? This remark thus reflects the attitude of respect toward older people that one would expect in a member of Jewish society at the time of Jesus.

Luke 14:12-14 provides some important information about the recipients of the service Jesus demands of his followers: When one gives a banquet, friends, relatives, and rich neighbors should not be the guests but rather "the poor, the maimed, the lame, the blind" (today the list easily could include "the elderly"). Jesus thus suggested that the kind of service God will repay "at the resurrection of the just" is precisely that which one renders to those who cannot repay it on earth. To "serve" the wealthy and the powerful does not require much out of the ordinary (indeed, such behavior is often in reality "*self*-serving"), but to put oneself into the role of servant to those who are considered the dregs of society represents something closer to Jesus' actions and more in line with his demands.

When supplemented by the more specific teachings of the New Testament concerning respect and care for the elderly, especially for one's parents, the demands for Christians to love others as Christ first loved them and to be servants of all provide a clear mandate to those today seeking scriptural guidance on the question of obligations toward the elderly.

General Concern for the Disadvantaged

The centrality of love and service in the ethic of Jesus finds clear demonstration in his concern for those who are disadvantaged for any reason. The Gospel picture of Jesus thus portrays him as one who indisputably stood firmly in his religious tradition in asserting a deep and keenly felt compassion for the unfortunates of the world. As chapter 2 showed, at the very heart of the religion of Israel lay a divinely ordained obligation to protect and to provide for those unable to do so for themselves, especially widows, orphans, strangers, and (the evidence suggests) the elderly, particularly one's own parents as they grow older. This obligation definitely has *religious* roots that stem from the creation of all human beings in God's own image, the development of a community among those who share a common relationship with God, and Yahweh's care for the people of Israel when they were weak and helpless.

All these elements underlie the reported statements of Jesus on the subject, statements that find strong corroboration in his actions. The Sermon on the Plain in Luke drives the point home sharply when it begins with the blunt assertion, "Blessed are you poor, for yours is the kingdom of God" (6:20). Unlike the better known parallel in Matthew 5:3, Luke's version concerns itself not with the spiritual condition of the audience but rather with their economic state alone. In addition, when John the Baptist's disciples asked Jesus if he was the one "who is to come," his response made explicit what he considered to be proof of the Messiah's identity: "Go and tell John what you have seen and heard: the blind received their sight, the lame walk, lepers are cleansed, and the deaf hear, the dead are raised up, the poor have good news preached to them" (Lk. 7:22). Undeniably, then, the Gospels depict Jesus as a Messiah who had a special concern for the weak, the needy, and the neglected in society.

115

Nowhere is this aspect of Jesus' teaching more vividly expressed (or his continuity with the religio-ethical heart of Old Testament tradition more clearly shown) than in Matthew 25:31-46, the parable of the great judgment. In this familiar story, Jesus made clear that in the final judgment neither creedal orthodoxy nor cultic punctiliousness will determine one's eternal fate, but rather the concern and the assistance (firsthand, or better, "hands-on") that one has rendered to society's unfortunates. Especially significant in this parable is the fact that Jesus clearly identified *himself* (assuming that he was speaking of himself here) with "the least of these my brethren." To offer assistance to one of these needy ones is to offer it to the Son of man himself, a fact that Christians say points once again to the importance of "the image of God" within every human being. Aid rendered to another person who reflects God's image (and especially to a needy one) is aid rendered to the incarnate God himself.

There can be little disagreement that many older people in America are members of the class of downtrodden, neglected, and needy people about whom Jesus was speaking in this parable and for whose welfare the Lord of Judgment will hold others accountable. Significantly, that Jesus did not include the aged in his lists of those needing special attention may reflect the essentially positive situation and role of the elderly in Jewish society that was described in chapter 2. At any rate, if he were uttering the parable today, he surely could have included, "I was old, and you ignored me."

Of course, for Jesus true religion could not be reduced merely to good works but depended upon a particular relationship with God. This relationship, however, leads necessarily to a certain attitude in one's dealings with one's fellows, as Jesus made clear in the Sermon on the Mount (and elsewhere): "Every sound tree bears good fruit, but the bad tree bears evil fruit. . . . Thus you will know them by their fruits" (Mt. 7:17, 20). The conclusion is hard to avoid that for Jesus there is a very close connection between one's inner relationship with God and one's outer relationship with one's fellow men and women.

Specific Statements About the Elderly

Jesus thus reaffirmed and demonstrated the concern expressed in the Old Testament for the disadvantaged and neglected members of society, and he made his followers' treatment of them a virtual test of their relationship with God. Later canonical commentators continued this theme, amplified by Jesus' emphasis upon love for others expressed in servanthood. This more general concern for the needy also finds expression specifically with regard to older members of the community.

RESPECT   As did the Old Testament, so also the New Testament expects the basic attitude toward the elderly (especially parents) to be one of respect and consideration. When Jesus called his disciples, the Gospel writers stressed that they left everything behind to follow him (cf. the discussion below of Jesus' statements about the family). As Vincent Taylor observes concerning Mark 1:20, "The completeness of the response [of James and John] is expressed by saying that they left their father Zebedee in the boat with the hired servants and went away with Jesus."[8] That Mark stated explicitly that the young men left *even* their father behind to follow Jesus clearly indicates the importance of the respect due to one's father, not to mention the societal expectation to care for one's parents when they became old.

Paul vividly demonstrates the same attitude in his brief letter to Philemon concerning a runaway slave. Verses 8-10 read:

> Accordingly, though I am bold enough in Christ to
> command you to do what is required, yet for love's sake I
> prefer to appeal to you—I, Paul, [an old man⁹] and now a
> prisoner also for Christ Jesus—I appeal to you for my child,
> Onesimus, whose father I have become in my
> imprisonment.

Obviously Paul assumed that age in and of itself commands respect and obedience. Why else would he have chosen this particular characteristic to mention in the same sentence in which he finally got to the point of his letter: "I appeal to you for my child, Onesimus, whose father I have become in my imprisonment"? Paul thus asked Philemon to forgive Onesimus inasmuch as they were now brothers, not only because they had the same Lord and heavenly Father (v. 16), but also because they had the same earthly spiritual father, who is now an "old man" as well!

Further explicit evidence for the respect accorded the elderly occurs elsewhere. The author of 1 Peter, for example, after a series of instructions to the elders of the church, states, "Likewise you that are younger be subject to the elders" (5:5). Although this statement does not contradict what has been said previously about the evolution of the word "elder" into a term for an office without necessary regard for age, it does clearly indicate that at least in some instances the elders were actually older, and that the younger members of the congregation were to defer to them not only because of their rank but also because of their age. It is not surprising that in a partriarchal, traditional society, the older members would be invested with the positions of leadership. Here the writer is reminding the younger, perhaps impatient Christians that those who have lived longer are generally wiser and less inclined to make hasty and ill-advised decisions. It should be noted, however, that the mutuality seen in several other New Testament writings appears here also: The verse continues, "Clothe

yourselves, *all of you*, with humility toward one another"
(emphasis added).

In 1 Timothy 5:1-2, the young minister is told, "Do not
rebuke an older man but exhort him as you would a father;
treat younger men like brothers, older women like mothers,
younger women like sisters, in all purity." Clearly the younger
members of the church were not excluded from positions of
authority, and there were times when they had to correct older
members. But they were to do so not with harsh, disrespectful
words but in positive, supportive ways, remembering the
honor and the respect always due to those who were older.
Here again the basic Christian principles of love toward
others and equality before God find application and
illustration with regard to obligations toward the elderly.

MATERIAL SUPPORT FOR THE ELDERLY   As examination of the
fifth commandment in the Old Testament Decalogue
demonstrated, the respect accorded older members of the
community, especially one's elderly parents, did not consist
merely of showing deference and politeness to them. It also
included a requirement to meet their physical needs when
they were unable to do so. Not surprisingly, the early
Christian church reflected this same concern, and in doing
so it followed Jesus' example in a controversy recorded by
Mark and Matthew.

The Synoptic Gospels record a number of disputes that
Jesus had with the scribes and the Pharisees, including this
important one concerning "the traditions of the elders"
(Mk. 7:1-23; cf. Mt. 15:1-20), that is, the rabbinical
commentary upon Torah. The controversy began when the
Jewish religious leaders questioned the failure of Jesus and
his followers to perform the proper ritual ablutions before
eating. In typical fashion Jesus responded by quoting their
own Scriptures and pointing out the hypocrisy in their
commitment to "the tradition of men" at the expense of

"the commandment of God" (Mk. 7:8-9). He then illustrated the general point by citing a particular instance that is of great significance to this study: By quoting the fifth commandment and Exodus 21:17 ("He who speaks evil of father or mother, let him surely die"), Jesus affirmed the Law's statement, in both positive and negative form, of the obligation to honor and care for parents. Apparently, however, rabbinic tradition held that uttering a certain oath would allow one to say to one's parents, "The support you could have expected from me is Corban (that is, given to God)," enabling one then to withhold from them the only means of support they reasonably could have expected for their old age.

The exact circumstances to which Jesus was referring in Mark 7:11-12 are difficult to determine. "Corban" may refer to an early example of some kind of *inter vivos* trust, in which control of a person's property was handed over to the religious authorities on the condition that during one's lifetime one would continue to receive "income" from it. The purpose of the vow as Jesus cited it, however, seemed to be specifically the non-support of parents, a dereliction which suggests that anger toward the parents (prompted by a quarrel perhaps?) might have been behind the son's action. At any rate, dedication "to God" in all likelihood meant "to the temple"; so in addition to denying divinely commanded support to elderly parents, the scribes' insistence on the Corban vow bore a hint of self-aggrandizement as well.

In fact, the precise meaning and use of the term "Corban" are not of great importance here; what is crucial is Jesus' *response* to those who used the concept to avoid their responsibility to their aging parents. Whatever the exact situation, Jesus' point is clear: The scribes and the Pharisees, zealous to uphold the sacredness of a vow, were ignoring and thus negating the truly sacred, that is, the will of God as expressed in the Law.

Jesus' primary purpose in this interchange evidently was to affirm the priority of the word of God over any and every human interpretation of it (and perhaps especially interpretations that appeared to be ecclesiastically self-serving).[10] For this purpose any number of scribal practices would have served as well (and did on other occasions). The fact that Mark depicts Jesus, at a crucial point in his career, as having his first real argument with the religious authorities over this matter of the Corban vow is therefore noteworthy. Other passages reveal a variety of areas in which Jesus thought the Pharisees had substituted their human traditions for God's will; yet support for older parents was the issue that Jesus used to illustrate his position and to make a clear and irrevocable break with tradition. The obvious conclusion is that this was an issue about which he felt strongly and wanted to make his position known. Furthermore, the fact that the tradition preserved *this* particular incident, and that Mark used it to illustrate Jesus' differences with (and from) the Pharisees, suggests that the content of the matter was important to the early church as well.

That the early church understood that Jesus did not merely preach concern for one's older parents but practiced it himself finds illustration in an incident from Jesus' life recorded by John. This story not only serves as a concrete example of the point Jesus was making in the passage just considered but also reinforces the claim made above that fulfilling the fifth commandment was an obligation Jesus took very seriously. John reports (19:26-27) that as Jesus hung dying on the cross, he saw his mother standing with the beloved disciple. Even in the agony of the moment, he made provision for her care and thus fulfilled the traditional responsibility of the eldest son who had become the head of the family. Although the new relationship was one of mutuality—"Woman, behold, your son! . . . Behold, your mother!"—the disciple took on the care of Mary, an action suggesting that this was the expected, appropriate, and natural response to Jesus' charge to him to "become" Mary's son: "And from that hour the disciple took her to his own home."[11] For Christians who find in the Gospel portrayal of Jesus a model for their own behavior, the message that John conveys here seems clear.

CONCERN ABOUT WIDOWS Jesus' provision for the care of his mother is reflected in a specific area in the New Testament in which the question of obligations toward the elderly comes to the fore, namely, its concern about *widows*. Chapter 2 discussed the emphasis that the Old Testament placed upon caring for the poor, especially the widow and the orphan (e.g., Ex. 22:21-24), and the early Christians took this responsibility seriously. James 1:27 states, "Religion that is pure and undefiled before God and the Father is this: to visit orphans and widows in their affliction, and to keep oneself unstained from the world." The author certainly did not intend to reduce the Christian faith to something so limited; but he was following the Law and the prophets and Jesus himself in stating that regular worship and cultic observance were inadequate without an active expression of the inner fruits of one's relationship with God (cf. Mic. 6:8; Mk. 12:28-34). The concrete example he chose was concern for widows and orphans. "The 'affliction' to which James refers may be sickness or old age, in the case of widows; the orphan and widow through bereavement were usually poor and needed money and other practical help."[12] Whatever James may have meant, old age is such an "affliction," to which he would have wanted his readers to attend.

The primary scriptural sources of information about widows in the early church are 1 Timothy 5:3-16 and Acts 6:1. A consideration of these passages brings to light several important facts. First, the matter of definition arises, relevant here inasmuch as it pertains to the question of age.

Clearly there were "classes" of widows in the church, with three (or possibly four) mentioned in 1 Timothy 5. Apparently, "real widows" were those who were "left all alone" and had no relatives whatsoever to assist in their care and support (cf. v. 16), which was an expected responsibility on the part of family members (cf. vv. 4, 8, 16). Although there is no explicit statement that widows who deserve care are necessarily *old*, the clear implication of the distinction between "real widows" and "younger widows" (v. 11) leads to such a conclusion.[13] Martin Dibelius and Hans Conzelmann thus seem justified in their conclusion that the "true widow" of verse 3 is "probably the same as the 'widow' " of verse 9, that is, the widow who is to be enrolled at sixty.[14] Whatever decision one reaches about the *age* implied by the term "widow," the fact remains that the New Testament gives an unequivocal mandate to care for those who have lost their husbands. Certainly this mandate applies to *elderly* widows, and especially to one's *own* widowed mother, as the rest of the passage makes clear.

First Timothy 5:4, 8, and 16 are particularly significant in this regard. In addition to removing the younger widows from the roll of "real widows" who can expect the "honor" (i.e., support) of the church, the author also excludes those widows who have families.[15] Given the general family situation of the time, as well as the Jewish emphasis on providing for parents in their old age, such an exclusion is not surprising. But it is worthy of note by Christians today who want to live in accord with the dictates of the canonical Scriptures of their faith. The clear message of 1 Timothy is that children, grandchildren, and apparently even other relatives have a duty to take care of elderly widows.

Three motives for fulfilling this duty appear in the passage. First, to do so is presented as a "religious duty" which the children should learn (v. 4), hardly surprising given the prominence of the fifth commandment in Jewish life and thought: "If anyone does not provide for his relatives, and especially for his own family [note that these two phrases appear to extend the principle beyond only widows], he has disowned the faith and is worse than an unbeliever" (v. 8).

Next, younger members of the family should support older members in order to "make some return to their parents" (v. 4). To the specifically religious motive is added a more mundane but still important and legitimate one: repayment in some sense for the time, effort, expense, and pain expended on the children by those responsible for their rearing, who now are in a situation of need themselves.

Finally, verse 16 contains one last injunction to "any believing woman [or, according to other manuscripts, 'man or woman' or 'man'] who has relatives who are widows" to assist them so that "the church [may] not be burdened." The author speaks here as a good steward. The church did and still should help those who cannot help themselves, but resources were and always will be limited. This passage recognizes this reality and commands family members to provide help to their own so that the church can minister to the ones "left all alone." This probably worked a hardship on many, limiting what they could do with their money; thus this command was not easy to fulfill. Few of Christ's demands are.

Acts 6:1 provides a firsthand illustration of the church's obligation to "real widows." According to Acts 2:44-45 and 4:32-35, the earliest Christians, being "of one heart and soul," made a practice of selling their possessions, pooling their resources, and distributing out of this common fund "to each as any had need," with the result that "there was not a needy person among them." The "real widows"— those with no relatives to provide for them—obviously would have been among the neediest members of the group, and Acts 6:1 indicates that a daily distribution was made from the common fund to meet their needs. The Greek-speaking Jews of Jerusalem, however, felt that their widows were being neglected, and their protest led to the choice of "seven men of good repute" who were to free the twelve from the day-to-day administration of the relief fund (6:3). This vignette indicates that providing for the needs of the widows was a serious matter indeed in the early church.

Sayings of Jesus That Appear to Disparage the Family   Before leaving this look at New Testament expressions of concern for the elderly, one further matter needs consideration: Scattered throughout Jesus' teachings in the Synoptics are several that seem to belittle family ties and obligations and thus could be used by some Christians to justify their failure to respond to the needs of aged parents (and, by extrapolation, of others). All of these statements, however, are open to a common and straightforward explanation that, if anything, actually serves to *heighten* Jesus' expression of the importance of such relationships. The sayings in question fall into two basic categories: (1) those in which Jesus appears to deny his own family (Mk. 3:31-35 and parallels); and (2) those in which he demands that his followers forsake and even "hate" various relatives (Mt. 10:34-39; Lk. 9:59-62; 14:25-27; cf. Mt. 19:29). The explanation of both of these groups of sayings rests upon a recognition of Jesus' fundamental message and self-understanding.

The central theme of Jesus' preaching was the coming of the kingdom of God, as announced in the first words of his public ministry (Mk. 1:15) and strongly reiterated in the Sermon on the Mount (Mt. 6:33). One of the key aspects of the kingdom was the absolute supremacy of its claims upon the *whole* life of the believer (cf. the parables of the kingdom in Mt. 13:44-45, in which the kingdom is likened to a "treasure in a field" and a "pearl of great value," for which the finders will sell all they have).

In this context, both groups of sayings mentioned above yield a considerably different meaning from that which might first appear to be the case. Jesus was not denying family ties or the natural relationships of life, nor was he demanding the cessation of natural affection for relatives as a condition for following him. Rather, he was merely asserting that *if* conflicts occur (as his own experience apparently led him to realize was likely),[16] loyalty to the kingdom of God must take precedence—even if it comes down to a choice between natural, human affections and God's will.[17] This view finds support in Luke's inclusion of the phrase, "yes, and even his own life," after the list of relatives one must "hate" (14:26). The entire utterance about "hating" relatives thus appears in the broader context of Jesus' continual stress on losing one's life in order to find it (the very point which concludes the section in Matthew's version). Whatever one thinks Jesus meant by that "hard saying," it applies literally to very few people.

Although Jesus may have been disappointed by the lack of sympathy among his kinfolk for his mission (cf. Mk. 3:33), the statements about his "true" family do not imply that he cared nothing for natural family ties. His emphasis on doing the will of God, however, "sets family relationships on a new plane in which the ties of a common obedience to God are superior to those of blood."[18] It is not surprising, then—and quite significant for this study—that the saying "must have been hard for any Jew to receive, for whom the command 'Honor thy father and thy mother' was part of the Decalogue."[19]

In sum, in the difficult sayings of Jesus concerning family relationships and obligations, he was not disparaging the family or denying its various responsibilities.[20] Rather, he was setting *priorities* that must be acknowledged by those who would be his disciples: All other loyalties, ties, and duties had to be completely subordinate to following Jesus. If his call led to division within families, so be it. In fact, if necessary, everything had to be given up for the sake of the kingdom, including family ties and even one's very life. To be a disciple meant to recognize the kingdom's greater claim that only those who do the will of God are true members of Christ's family. So instead of devaluing the family in these sayings, Jesus tacitly acknowledged the high place that the family held in his thought by using family relationships in his examples of what God's claim upon his human creatures entails: When obedience to God's call requires it, *even* family relationships and duties—even those ties that should be the most intimate and precious on earth and those responsibilities that should be the weightiest—have to yield (cf. Abraham in Gen. 12:1-4). Indeed, this is the *ultimate* sacrifice for the kingdom's sake, worthy of mention in the same breath as giving up one's very life.

Summary

Concerning *attitudes toward aging,* the central Christian doctrine of the Incarnation reinforces two critical points affirmed by the Old Testament notion of creation "in the image of God": the value and the dignity of every human being, and the essential goodness of creation and thus of the human body. The writings of Paul provide further insight into the New Testament message concerning aging by developing some of the implications of the Incarnation for understanding one's body. Through his key distinction between *sarx* and *soma,* Paul contributes a means for Christians to come to grips with the deterioration of their bodies without losing a sense of self-worth.

In the Gospels, Jesus appears as one who urges people not to be unduly concerned about the physical conditions of life (including, by implication, the aging of their bodies) but to be greatly concerned about helping others maintain self-respect whatever their circumstances. The New Testament also reflects the attitude of the Old Testament that the elderly generally possess greater wisdom and therefore are worthy of special respect. Of particular interest is the place that the church gave to widows and other older people, who had specific and important responsibilities. As in the Old Testament, use of the term "elder" to designate the leaders of the church demonstrates at least a tacit belief that the elderly were specially qualified to hold positions of authority. Finally, the vision of Revelation 21 reiterates a theme that runs throughout the Bible: God can "make all things new," not only at the end of time but even in the here and now in the life of believers, a fact illustrated, for example, by the Gospel story of Nicodemus.

With regard to *obligations toward the elderly*, the message of the New Testament stands firmly in line with that of the Old Testament. The basic principle underlying all that the New Testament says on the matter is Jesus' command of love for others, a command echoed in numerous other places. Jesus himself continued the concern of the Law and the prophets for the weak and the needy, and he contributed his own vivid example of a living expression of this compassion.

Amplifying the general New Testament view that the elderly are worthy of special honor and respect, Jesus also maintained the Old Testament's demand for their material support: In an important controversy with the Pharisees concerning the vow of Corban, Jesus made clear that the divine command to honor and care for older parents cannot be set aside, even for a religious act such as dedicating one's property to God. That he himself was sensitive to this obligation is illustrated by his provision of care for his mother even as he hung dying on the cross.

Although the direct evidence is slight (perhaps because in Jewish society of his day the elderly's position was not particularly disadvantaged), the justifiable conclusion is that all that Jesus said and did is relevant for the aged in situations in which they are *not* treated with proper respect and care. The message of Jesus recorded in the Gospels leaves no room for neglect of the elderly (especially one's own parents) and actually demands an active concern for their well-being, indeed, for the welfare of all who are in any kind of need in one's community.

That the early church so understood the teaching of their founder is shown by the demands for the care of widows, an especially clear illustration of what is expected of Christians, particularly of the family members of older people. Finally, although several statements of Jesus may appear to undermine family responsibilities, when seen in their proper context they actually serve to heighten his expression of such obligations.

NOTES

1. A full consideration of this vast topic is beyond the scope of this book. The classic work in English on the subject remains J. A. T. Robinson's *The Body: A Study in Pauline Theology* (London: S.C.M. Press, 1952). For a more recent bibliography (and further helpful information), see Robert Jewett, "Body," in Keith Crim et al., eds., *The Interpreter's Dictionary of the Bible*, supplementary volume (Nashville: Abingdon Press, 1976), pp. 117-18. In the discussion that follows, all quotations are from Robinson, *The Body*. For the sake of simplicity, most page citations are in parentheses in the text.

2. Robinson, *The Body*, p. 31, italics in the original. He reiterates that Paul never suggests that *sarx* and *soma* "represent different *parts* of a man's make-up, and that one is mortal and the other not. Each stands for the whole man differently regarded—man as wholly perishable, man as wholly destined for God" (pp. 31-32).

3. Indeed, aging can help to facilitate the necessary shift from a *sarx*-determined existence to a *soma*-determined one. That is, as one grows older, one is less and less able to live according to one's *own* will (often directed to less desirable ends) because one's body is no longer so clearly and easily one's own (in the sense of performing up to one's wishes and at one's bidding). A clear example might be the athlete's loss of abilities with age, when the person simply no longer can do what he or she did with ease when younger. To anticipate one of the theses of chapter 4, one can even say that aging thus leads to a recognition of finitude and limitation, forcing one to acknowledge dependence upon God as the source of one's true being and to surrender one's will to God.

4. A word is in order here about the approach this book will take to the numerous parallels that occur among the Synoptic Gospels: In order to avoid cluttering the text and/or creating a nightmare of notes, parallels will be listed only where there is reason to do so. Virtually all good modern editions of the Bible provide cross-references for easy consultation of parallels.

5. John Chrysostom, *On the Priesthood*, 3.16, trans. W. R. W. Stevens, in *A Select Library of the Nicene and Post-Nicene Fathers of the Christian Church*, ed. Philip Schaff, first series, vol. 9 (reprint, Grand Rapids, Mich.: Wm. B. Eerdmans, 1978), pp. 55-56. He goes on to urge the "superintendent" of the widows to "endure all these things in a generous spirit" because "this class of persons deserve to be pitied for their misfortunes, not to be insulted; and to trample upon their calamities, and add the pain of insult to that which poverty brings, would be an act of extreme brutality." All in all, this passage presents a rather dismal picture of the condition of widows at that time.

6. The use of the Fourth Gospel to illustrate Jesus' words and actions unquestionably raises special problems beyond those discussed earlier about the Gospels in general. John is even more interpretive and theological than the other evangelists and therefore in modern terms even less historical. Still, the early church obviously accepted his interpretation, and with regard to the concerns of this study, his writings certainly do not contradict the depiction of Jesus in the Synoptics.

7. Wolfgang Schrage, "Ethics in the NT," in Crim, *Interpreter's Dictionary*, supplementary volume, p. 285.

8. Vincent Taylor, *The Gospel According to St. Mark* (London: Macmillan, 1959), p. 170.

9. The RSV renders the word "old man" as "ambassador," a possibility in the Greek for which a case can be made. Paul, however, has just expressly assured Philemon that he was appealing to him "for love's sake" and was relinquishing his apostolic authority to "command"; it makes no sense, then, that in the same sentence he would refer to himself as an "envoy" or "ambassador," a clear allusion to delegated authority from one's sovereign. Eduard Lohse's conclusion (*Colossians and Philemon*, Hermeneia, trans. William R. Poehlmann and Robert J. Karris [Philadelphia: Fortress Press, 1971], p. 199) is therefore appropriate: Paul, in calling himself a *presbutes*, "is alluding to his age. . . . If Paul calls attention to his age and his imprisonment, he can expect that Philemon will pay due respect to his words."

10. Vincent Taylor (*Mark*, p. 339) asserts that "there can be no reasonable doubt that the words were spoken by Jesus and illustrate his attitude to the oral law." Indeed, the whole question of Jesus and the Law is a fascinating one. Underlying his freedom with regard to the Law clearly lay an acceptance of it—properly interpreted and applied—as the revealed will of God (cf. Mt. 5:17-20). In Mk. 10:19, e.g., in response to the rich man's question about inheriting eternal life, Jesus directed the man's attention to the portion of the Decalogue dealing with human personal relationships, including the commandment to "honor your father and mother." Obviously Jesus found there the basic norms for human conduct and relationship with God. As Taylor (p. 340) states concerning the Corban controversy, "A point of no small importance is that, while oral tradition is assailed by Jesus, the law in the Decalogue is accepted by Him as binding: what God said through Moses stands." Brevard Childs (*The Book of Exodus: A Critical, Theological Commentary* [Philadelphia: Westminster Press,

1974], p. 430) similarly concludes that "for Jesus, the Messiah, the law of Sinai is still unquestionably the will of God for Israel and for his disciples."

11. The Greek is literally "to his own" (neuter), not "to his own home." Perhaps "took her to his own" is even more expressive of what Jesus had in mind than "took her to his own home."

12. James Adamson, *The Epistle of James*, The New International Commentary on the New Testament (Grand Rapids, Mich.: Wm. B. Eerdmans, 1976), p. 86. The conclusion of Robert Butler (*Why Survive? Being Old in America* [New York: Harper & Row, 1975], p. 29) about contemporary American society has probably been valid throughout history: "Widows, single women and members of minority groups are particularly disadvantaged." He quotes Dr. Juanita Kreps, a leading economist, who says, "The older woman is the poorest in society today."

13. The context lends strong support to this interpretation: The discussion of "honoring" widows (note the linguistic similarity to the fifth commandment's "Honor your father and mother") follows immediately upon the injunction not to "rebuke an older man but exhort him as you would a father" and to treat "older women like mothers" (5:1-2). Perhaps the letter writer's thoughts were turned to the needy women of the church (primarily the aged widows) by the reference here to older men and women.

14. Martin Dibelius and Hans Conzelmann, *The Pastoral Epistles*, Hermeneia, trans. Philip Buttolph and Adela Yarbro (Philadelphia: Fortress Press, 1972), p. 74. Pertinent to a matter that this study has considered is their statement that the passage illustrates the development of a common word (which could still be used to describe anyone who had lost her husband) into a technical term to denote an "office" in the church, namely, "widows of the congregation." They conclude, "The situation is very similar to that of '*elder*'" (emphasis added).

15. Dibelius and Conzelmann (*Pastoral Epistles*, p. 74) comment on 1 Tim. 5:4: "If a widow has a family, then she has no need of such honors by the church (see v. 3). Rather, before the relatives devote themselves to other works of love, they should first of all 'show piety toward their own family, etc.'" (Punctuated as in source.)

16. That such conflicts actually occurred from the beginning of Christian history may be reflected in such passages as Mk. 13:12 (the parallel in Mt. 10:21-22, significantly, is part of the context for the statements of vv. 34-39). These sayings fit the common apocalyptic expectation for the "end times" as discussed in chapter 2 (cf., e.g., Is. 3:5 and Mic. 7:6), showing once again that respect for parents was so deeply rooted in Hebrew thought that lack of it became one of the major signs of the imminent end of civilization.

17. As the discussion of the Corban controversy made clear, however, Jesus was well aware that religion could be misused to avoid important responsibilities. Mk. 7:9-13 shows that the "call" must be genuine and the opposition real before one can claim release from family obligations; one cannot use "religious duty" as an excuse to ignore needy parents and to forsake other family duties.

18. Taylor, *Mark*, p. 247.

19. Frederick C. Grant, "St. Mark: Exegesis," in George A. Buttrick et al., *The Interpreter's Bible*, vol. 7 (Nashville: Abingdon Press, 1951), p. 694.

20. Jesus' special understanding of the father-son relationship and his application of it to himself and God are also relevant here (cf., e.g., Jn. 5:17-18): One who did not consider family ties important would hardly have made extensive use of precisely such a relationship, especially to make some very significant theological points.

131

CONCERNING
ATTITUDES
TOWARD AGING

CHAPTER FOUR

A survey of biblical materials that deal with aging and the elderly demonstrates that the Bible does not present a well-defined "theology of aging," much less a blueprint for "how to enjoy the Golden Years" or a social program for coping with the rapidly increasing number of elderly persons. In fact, as the previous two chapters have shown, Scripture does not even present a unified attitude toward aging (though concerning obligations to the elderly the witness is more uniform). The Bible nonetheless provides considerable information of great value to anyone who wishes to address these issues, and for those who stand in faith within the biblical tradition, its perspective is crucial. An attempt must be made now to use the knowledge gained in the previous two chapters as a basis for addressing the issues concerning both aging itself and responsibilities toward the elderly as reviewed in chapter 1.

The Religious Response

The Problem with the Contemporary Christian Approach

Religious groups have begun to respond to the social changes outlined in chapter 1 and to the generally negative impact of these changes upon the self-image, role, and status of the elderly. Indeed, many Christian denominations in this country have as a major emphasis some aspect of "ministry to the aging." Journal articles and books pour forth offering guidance, inspiration, and resources for coping with aging and caring for the elderly.[1] Most of this Christian writing on aging has been overwhelmingly affirmative, emphasizing that aging is a process of fulfillment, maturity, and completion, and old age a time to be eagerly awaited and warmly embraced.

For example, the highly regarded book by Henri J. M. Nouwen and Walter J. Gaffney, *Aging: The Fulfillment of Life*, well illustrates the point in both its title and its contents:

We believe that aging is the most common human experience which overarches the human community as a rainbow of promises. . . . It is so filled with promises that it can lead us to discover more and more of life's treasures. We believe that aging is not a slow decaying but a gradual maturing, not a fate to be undergone but a chance to be embraced.[2]

Another good illustration is found in Alfons Deeken's book, *Growing Old, and How to Cope with It:*

133

I will try to show that old age, far from being an embarrassment, is in fact a golden opportunity for human growth, fulfillment, and deep happiness. . . . It is hoped that in the future more and more senior citizens will discover the unique opportunities that old age can offer them and that some will even begin to see for themselves that "Old is beautiful!"[3]

All of these hopes for "senior citizens" are unquestionably commendable and diligently to be sought. That their experiences do not warrant such untempered optimism, however much people might *wish* they did, is equally undeniable. In reality, old age is simply not such a wonderful experience for most people, including those who do not live in poverty, loneliness, and neglect. Most of this material thus shares one fundamental failing: In the rush to be optimistic, supportive, and "pastoral," the writers refuse to take seriously the very real problems experienced by human beings as they grow older. This admirable approach to aging is therefore simply unrealistic in its presentation of the true nature of the aging phenomenon and Christianity's proper attitude toward it.[4]

It should be noted that this overly positive approach to the "joy of aging" is not limited to religious writings: Partly as a result of the effectiveness of the "Gray Power" movement in bringing about a more positive evaluation of the elderly, and partly as a corrective to past excesses in the other direction, the optimistic attitude toward aging has become the predominant "official" position of American society, leading to a situation in which anyone who points out the negative aspects of aging tends to be looked upon as ageist at worst or out of date at best.

An Alternative Approach: Discipleship of the Cross

A more realistic and therefore more helpful approach is one that acknowledges the losses associated with aging and deals with them as an inevitable if not a particularly welcome facet of human existence. The truth is that aging is the deterioration of the organism that *is* the human person, and deterioration, even if inevitable and universal, is hardly something that most people desire or welcome. This decline represents the loss of powers that were previously taken for granted, the loss of much that makes people who they are (or at least have always perceived themselves to be). Considerable pain unquestionably accompanies such loss—first, *emotional* pain, as friends and relatives, especially a beloved spouse, depart in death, and as one sees one's own powers and abilities fade; and second, *physical* pain, as more and more problems and ailments appear that have no pill or therapy to cure or even to ameliorate them.

Those who stand in the Christian tradition and presume to enlighten others about aging are thus doing older people a disservice by painting too golden a picture of old age, a picture that few elderly people will be able to achieve. What about the guilt that may be provoked in those who simply cannot get up each morning—however strong their faith and however hard they pray—and exclaim, "How wonderful it is to be alive another day!" because they are consumed with pain from arthritis or do not even know who and where they are? What of the spouse who has to watch a beloved partner of a half-century slowly decline to the point where that most heinous of acts—*killing* someone whom one loves—begins to look like an act of love? Is it possible that a little more reality in preachments about old age would be not only more honest but also more in line with authentic Christian faith?

Most Christian writing on aging, however, has failed to give sufficient attention to the realities of life as many people experience them. Instead, Christian authors (understandably enough, one must grant) have tended to write from the perspective of the Resurrection, stressing the hope to which

135

Christians can cling by virtue of the saving work of Christ: "Have no fear of growing old," these sources say, "of losing the abilities and powers that our society constantly says give you worth—just on the other side there is the New Day, the New Life you have been waiting for, where you will be given powers you never dreamed of!"[5]

Perhaps, however, for the sake of honesty and of credible witness to those who are actually experiencing it, aging and old age need to be looked at from the perspective of the cross. This approach seems to speak more accurately to the common experience of growing old, at least in the earthly, existential sense, than does the Resurrection (though for the Christian the Resurrection *does* always stand *beyond* the cross). Recent years have brought a more balanced assessment of the "beauty" or "dignity" of death through reminders that death for most people is not all that pleasant or desirable (however inevitable)[6]; similarly, the time has come to take a more realistic and honest look at the "glory of aging" as it is experienced by real, live human beings.

Such realism appears to have been the dominant view in the early Christian communities (not surprisingly, given the circumstances that gave them their beginning). Jesus is never depicted as promising that life would be painless and free from struggle[7]; indeed, his message seems to be the opposite: "In the world you have tribulation."[8] As Martin Marty has put it, "The prophets, Jesus, the apostles, spoke and acted as if it would be uphill all the way. If the world 'naturally' was where they thought God wanted it to be, then why expect 'supranatural' intervention, in the form of prophetic inspiration, the Incarnation, or whatever?"[9]

What might a contemporary Christian, attempting to express this perspective, have to say to those who are growing older? How might he or she address their needs better than by merely offering encouragement and exhortation to look on the bright side of things? To consider

136

aging and old age from the perspective of the cross means at least to take seriously the call of Jesus in passages such as Luke 9:23-24: "If any man would come after me, let him deny himself and take up his cross daily and follow me. For whoever would save his life will lose it; and whoever loses his life for my sake, he will save it." The implications of this "hard saying" for a Christian view of aging are numerous and profound, and its application in a particular individual's life will depend on a number of factors. What follows is only a general outline that each person must adapt to her or his own unique situation, self-understanding, and beliefs.

Hans Küng, in his classic *On Being a Christian*, goes straight to the heart of the matter: "Discipleship is always—sometimes in a hidden way, sometimes openly—a discipleship of suffering, a following of the cross."[10] He points out that suffering is inherent in human existence and thus must be accepted. What distinguishes the Christian's acceptance of suffering, though, is the particular attitude one holds toward it—not an attitude of cultic adoration, mystical union, or ethical imitation, but rather one of "correlation, of correspondence" with the way in which Jesus dealt with his own suffering (p. 576). Significantly, this approach means that "anyone who wants to go with Jesus must deny *himself* and take on himself, not the cross of Jesus nor just any kind of cross, but his cross, his own cross." Küng concludes with a statement full of possibilities for a realistic Christian view of aging:

> But what is required of the person who believes in the crucified Jesus is something that frequently recurs and is therefore mostly more difficult than a single heroic act: it is the endurance of *ordinary, normal, everyday* suffering, which is then most likely to prove excessive. The cross to be borne is therefore the cross of everyday life. That this is far from being obvious or edifying is apparent to anyone who has seen how often a person tries to get away from his own cross,

all his daily obligations, demands, claims, promises in his family or his calling; how he tries to shift his cross onto others or suppress it altogether. (p. 577, emphasis added)

Suffering of course takes many forms, but one of the "crosses" of everyday life that Christian Americans are expected to bear is surely renunciation of attachment to the "things of this world"—more difficult now than it ever has been, given contemporary society's materialism and reliance on external criteria as determinants of one's personal value. One important aspect of this renunciation is the abandonment of dependence upon the opinions of others as the source of one's self-identity and self-worth, the refusal to let one's values be determined by such worldly standards as beauty, wealth, power, status, and yes, even youth. As a later section will make clear, the Christian faith affirms that God's standards are very different (cf. 1 Cor. 1:18-31).

Aging, then, and the various kinds of suffering it inevitably brings with it can be seen in a paradoxical way (and what is more characteristic of Christianity than paradox?) as contributing to one's Christian growth, maturity, indeed, even Christ-likeness. As Dietrich Bonhoeffer so bluntly put it, "When Christ calls a man, he bids him come and die."[11] So it is that the losses of aging—strength, mobility, physical attractiveness, sociability, the opportunity to make continued contributions to society—perhaps these losses are just another manifestation of the cross that Christ has held out to his followers ever since he called his first disciples, the cross that indeed is the *only* means by which one ever will be a true disciple. It is, in fact, only through loss of all that one previously valued as the "old creation" that the new creation in Christ (2 Cor. 5:17) can come into existence (as Paul suggests in 1 Cor. 15 by using the imagery of the seed's death as prerequisite to the plant's life).

ACKNOWLEDGMENT OF DEPENDENCE   The ultimate meaning of this understanding of discipleship as suffering, as daily taking up one's cross in the normal setbacks of human existence, is in fact that which has made the cross of Christ such a scandal (or at least stumbling block) for so many through the centuries. If one accepts the central Christian doctrine that the death of Jesus Christ alone is sufficient to restore the relationship between God and his human creatures, then one must acknowledge one's absolute dependence on the unmerited and freely offered grace of God. Indeed, the real root of contemporary Americans' inability to come to terms with growing older may lie right here, at the heart of the "human problem" as described by Christianity for two thousand years and by Judaism for several millennia before that. Perhaps the denial of aging—illustrated, for example, by efforts to overcome the loss of youth through whatever means possible and by the growing tendency to institutionalize those whose care is a burden[12]—is only one more example of the human desire to "make it on our own," to "do it our way," to refuse to accept the limitations and the finitude inherent in creaturehood.

Mac and Anne Turnage express the point well in one of the fictional letters that make up their *Graceful Aging: Biblical Perspectives:* "Perhaps the most miserable, the ultimate role change is to dependence! Is that what makes aging such a threat? Honestly, I don't know how I can handle it if I become a burden."[13] William F. May offers corroboration from a sociological and historical perspective when, after noting that "the aged remind the middle aged of their own imminent destiny," he says:

> What the middle aged fear, however, is not merely physical decay, the loss of beauty, and the failure of vitality, but the humiliation of dependency. Americans have historically taken pride in themselves as an independent people

139

> . . . . The dark side of this aspiration to self-reliance is an abhorrence of dependency. . . . The North American compulsion to be independent intensifies the threat of old age. The middle aged do not want the elderly to encumber them, and the elderly do not want to lapse into a burden.[14]

What May observes from a secular perspective about middle-aged Americans today, the biblical tradition has long affirmed from a theological vantage about the human race in general, from its very beginning. That is, the problem with aging in late twentieth-century America seems to be only another in the long run of reprises of that drama played out at the dawn of time in the mythical garden of Genesis 3, namely, the unwillingness of human beings to be satisfied with merely being "in the *image* of God" and their desire instead to be *like* God, that is, independent, not beholden to anyone, *self*-sufficient. The refusal to accept the limits that define human freedom is the primordial sin that led the first couple astray, and aging certainly is a limit that many Americans are refusing to accept. In short, Americans do not like getting old because it forces them into a situation that is at the very heart of the "human problem"—the necessity of facing the fact that one is not self-sufficient and able to "go it alone."

In a way matched only by seriously debilitating injury or illness (which are not nearly so common in human experience), aging is thus a *model* of what Christianity says it means merely to be a human being. That is, in the process of growing older one is *forced* to confront the fact that one is finite, unable to be and do all that one can imagine and desire. As J. R. P. Sclater observes:

> Old age has many compensations; but it is always a discipline. The process by which God pries our fingers loose from their clutch on things material is not entertaining. The closing of the doors of the senses, the

increasing feebleness of the physical powers, and the pathetic loneliness of great age make up a process of detachment which is stern in its mercy (cf. the frank depression of Eccl. 11:7-8).[15]

Little wonder that contemporary Americans are having so much trouble dealing with their own aging and coping with the rapidly increasing number of older people all around them.

At its very heart, though, Christianity is all about being dependent, accepting that one does not live on one's own and only for oneself at *any* point in life, not just when one grows old. Paul's great statement captures the essence of what Christianity claims is both the problem of and the solution to the human condition: "It is no longer I who live, but Christ who lives in me" (Gal. 2:20). If one can assimilate the fact that one is totally dependent throughout life upon the creating, redeeming, and sustaining God, then perhaps it will be easier to accept increasing dependence upon other human beings as one grows older. The problem humans *always* have to struggle with is precisely the difficulty of accepting the totally free grace of God (which is nothing more than acknowledging utter dependence upon God).

All of this means, of course, that Christians do not need to deny the very real losses involved in growing older. Throughout its history, Christianity has insisted that the suffering of Jesus was totally real. Indeed, the denial of the reality of Jesus' suffering—the Docetic claim that he only *seemed* to suffer and to die—was explicitly condemned as one of the most dangerous of the early heresies that threatened Christianity. No, Christians acknowledge the reality and pain of their losses, and the reality and pain become marks of identification with Christ and a sign of communion with him as a true disciple.

A more realistic and truthful approach to aging, then, and

one more in line with authentic Christian teaching, will not try to minimize the negative aspects of growing older and its inevitable losses. Along with all the reasons cited earlier (cf. chapter 1 especially) for denying one's own aging—and therefore in all likelihood devaluing those who remind one of what is happening to oneself—the primordial human tendency to want to be self-sufficient, to assert one's independence, to show that one can make it on one's own leads to efforts to sugarcoat the harsh realities of aging that demonstrate one's finitude. An honest Christian approach to the subject, on the other hand, will acknowledge the reality, will accept the aging person where he or she really is, and thus will not demand that the person deny what he or she knows from experience is true.

Of course, some Christians may object that the position just outlined goes *against* the teachings of Christianity by failing to be ever positive, hopeful, and cheerful, whatever one's circumstances in life. The tradition of expressing one's displeasure with the way life is going, however, is evident throughout the Bible, especially in the Old Testament. Job's cursing of the day of his birth is well known (3:1-26), and a surprising number of the psalms qualify as "psalms of complaint" (e.g., 55, 60, 64, 69, 70, 74, 88, and many others; cf. Is. 63:17 for a prophetic example). Luke depicts Jesus as giving at least implicit sanction to the legitimacy of complaining, in the parable of the unjust judge (Lk. 18:1-8), in which a widow's importunate advances carry the day even with an unrighteous judge (and, as Jesus makes clear, God is just). Paul says of the mysterious "thorn in the flesh" that three times he asked God for its removal (2 Cor. 12:7-10). The narratives and the personal portraits that emerged from the faith of Israel and the early church show no inclination to disguise the inevitable problems of human existence.

Further Contributions

An alternative Christian approach to aging, then, interprets its inevitable losses in light of a theology of the Cross that can lead to acknowledgment of dependence upon God, an acknowledgment that is necessary for the restoration of the divine-human relationship. In addition to the fundamental change in perspective of the alternative approach just presented, the biblical tradition can offer several other helpful insights into the meaning of the aging process and how to cope with it.

The Importance of the Body

One of the main reasons Christians can take a legitimate interest in the losses associated with aging, even to the point of acknowledging and complaining about bodily decline, is found in the central theological doctrine of the faith. As chapter 3 showed, the fact of the Incarnation means that the body *is* important, and its deterioration is a loss that one can legitimately and appropriately lament. Christians affirm that by becoming a human being, God himself ennobled the body (which, one must remember, Gen. 1 asserts that he had also created and judged "very good"). Christianity thus has no basis for devaluing the body or teaching that what happens to the body does not matter. Although disparagement of the body has appeared in Christian teaching all too often, to accept such a view as valid is to return to the Gnostic dualism with which the early church struggled so bitterly. The body *does* matter, and, as pointed out above, Christians can rightly regret the fading of the body's powers and abilities.

This message is important, because aging is primarily and basically a *bodily* phenomenon for most Americans, whose response to the question What is aging? is simply, "The

143

body begins to wear out and finally breaks down" (a view that, significantly, reflects contemporary culture's concept of the body as a *machine*). The development of such an attitude is not surprising. Society emphasizes the physical appearance and vigor of youth so much that they tend to become the central factors in determining one's self-image and sense of self-worth; and one certainty of aging is that the body *will* undergo fairly predictable (and unavoidable) changes. As the Old Testament recognized (most explicitly in Eccles. 12), the reflexes slow, the senses become less acute, the hair grays (or worse, disappears entirely!), youthful pleasures lose their appeal, and on and on. In this view, the real problem with getting old is simply that the body deteriorates, bringing on the humiliation of losing control over the functions (both "vital" and "rational"[16]) that contemporary culture says give people value as human beings (and indeed, in the view of increasing numbers of people, define one's very "humanhood"). Whatever one might believe about the survival of the soul in some kind of hereafter—and however much comfort such beliefs can bring—for most people today aging is first and foremost a physical, bodily matter.

THE HUMAN BEING AS MORE THAN BODY   The body of course *is* necessary for a human being to exist; as has been widely affirmed for some time now, in a fundamental sense the human being does not *have* a body but rather *is* a body.[17] Christianity, however, asserts with equal emphasis that the body is not totally definitive of the person (recall the discussion of human creation in "the image of God" in chapter 2). One surely cannot conceive of a "human" being in any intelligible sense of the word without a body, but *only* a body also fails to fulfill the common definition of "human." Thus the body (i.e., biological existence) may be said to be preconditional to, but not definitive of, personal existence. The body and its actions can reveal the "self " (indeed, are the only vehicle for self-revelation), but the self nonetheless remains more than *just* the body. In sum, what one is and who one is cannot be separated; but to say what one is, is not the last word in saying who one is.

This topic is impossible to discuss without the use of a distinction that is necessary for the sake of explication but is artificial and misleading if the mutuality and interrelation-ship of "body" and "spirit" are not kept clearly in mind. The body is necessary for the expression of the self—the "person"—but the body only discovers its real reason for existence as the personality uses it for self-expression. To use a biblical metaphor, as Christ is to the church (cf. Eph. 4:15-16; 5:23-24), so spirit is to the body; although each element is necessary, the relationship is not absolutely mutual. To stress the necessity of embodiment for personal existence, then, "is not to say that who we are *as persons* is defined by either primary or exclusive reference to our bodies, or that our personhood does not transcend in important ways the limitations imposed by our bodies."[18] This perspective is of course closely akin to the biblical concept of the psychophysical unity of the human being, and its implications for attitudes toward aging (especially as it affects the body) are apparent.

The True Basis of Personal Value: Being, Not Having

Whereas in the past the dominance of religious interests in society led to a tendency to devalue the physical aspect of the human being in favor of the spiritual component, today the opposite extreme has gained ascendancy. A general loss of interest in the spiritual aspects of life has occurred, accompanied by a decline of belief in a soul that survives the body. The physical nature of the human being thus has become all-important. This contemporary attitude toward the body is a manifestation of the more general approach to reality that can be called "materialism." As the physical body declines, the mortality that has always been a nagging problem for humans becomes an all-consuming problem: If the "body" is *all* that one has (or is), its decay is frightening indeed because it represents the total loss of the very self.

In the losses that inevitably accompany growing older, however, one is forced to look beyond the superficial, external determinants of worth so central to contemporary American society. The accepted view today is that one *is* what one *does*, that the basis of one's value is what one produces or contributes, almost always measured by some material standard. This view is the basis for today's "consumer society" ethic and leads individuals, in the words of Erich Fromm, to "identify themselves by the formula: *I am = what I have and what I consume.*"[19] As one ages, however, one undergoes a significant, twofold reduction: first, in what one *has* (in terms of physical attractiveness and vitality and of the ability to produce, which is the usual means for obtaining material possessions); and second, in what one can *consume* (in terms both of personal capacity to use and, for many elderly, of sufficient funds to buy what they might want). Thus in the consumer society old age must be seen by the aged themselves and by others observing them as a time of decreased value.

The root of the problem is, quite simply, that Americans receive a great deal of education in "having" but precious little in "being." When one reaches that stage of life when attention and energies are virtually forced to focus upon "being" rather than upon "having," one is little prepared for the assault upon one's self-image that such a change represents. As suggested above, however, this process, though painful, does not have to be all bad. James Whitehead points out the potential benefit with regard specifically to

146

retirement (and, incidentally, lends support to the call for a realistic Christian approach to aging advocated above):

> The social event of retirement performs a religiously ironic function: it empties out of a person's life perhaps the most sturdy crutch of self-worth, one's social role and usefulness. In this moment of stripping away, of death to a former style of life, the Church's ministry must not be that of substituting ersatz identities, but of celebrating this emptying process which leads to God.[20]

Evelyn Whitehead then concludes, "Stripped of these partial sources of identity, the religious person can grow to recognize, even celebrate, a deeper truth—that no one ever 'earns' his way, that life's meaning is more a gift than a reward." Reflecting the biblical teachings of the creation of all human beings in the image of God and of Christ's death for the sake of all, Christian theology has always strongly affirmed that one's value does not rest in what one *does* or *has* but in the fact that one *is*.

God's Different Standards

In 1 Corinthians 1:18-31, Paul gives expression to a basic Christian theological doctrine that is quite pertinent to this consideration of attitudes toward aging. He asserts that the Christian gospel is neither a philosophy accessible only to the wise nor a commodity available only to the wealthy and powerful. In fact, the fundamental requirement of the gospel is recognition that God has freely offered forgiveness to all; no effort of one's own is necessary (or even possible) to gain salvation (cf. Rom. 3:24). God thus chose the weak and the foolish, "according to worldly standards," as the vehicle of redemption, in order to demonstrate the insignificance of the "wisdom of the wise and the cleverness of the clever." Verses 26-29 state Paul's position most clearly:

> For consider your call, brethren; not many of you were wise according to worldly standards, not many were powerful, not many were of noble birth; but God chose what is foolish in the world to shame the wise, God chose what is weak in the world to shame the strong, God chose what is low and despised in the world, even things that are not, to bring to nothing things that are, so that no human being might boast in the presence of God.

The message of this passage is unmistakable: God's standards are different from those of the world.

The relevance of this point is clear. Granted, Paul did not refer to the elderly in his description of those through whom God chose to accomplish his will (again, perhaps because in his day and society they were not among the disadvantaged, or, as some have suggested, because early Christianity was primarily a "youth movement" and Paul's churches numbered few elderly people among their members); rather, he mentioned the foolish, the weak, the ignobly born. As chapter 1 showed, however, the elderly today fall into the same category of the "low and despised in the world"; and just as Paul's words must have given great encouragement to those whom society devalued in his day, so his message offers real hope to the aged who find their worth called into question in numerous ways today. The world still values and admires those who are "wise," "powerful," and "of noble birth"; added to this list are "young," "strong," "healthy," and "attractive." The Christian, however, has no reason to suppose that God has changed his standards, and the elderly can take comfort that God may want to use them to achieve some great (or small) end "so that no human being might boast in the presence of God."

That which God values and chooses to use to further his purposes, then, is often diametrically opposed to what the world considers significant and worthy of great ends (cf. Mt. 11:25). Furthermore, God is not at all impressed or deceived by external appearances or superficial differences (cf. Rom. 2:11). A sound body, therefore, is not required for acceptance by God. In the sacrificial scheme of Old Testament religion, the object offered to God had to be unblemished, perfect, in its prime, in order to be worthy. The heart of Christian theology, on the other hand, is the affirmation that the only perfect sacrifice, the most pleasing and acceptable body ever offered to God, was the crucified body of Jesus of Nazareth—a beaten, humiliated body that, whatever one's theory of atonement, is in some way responsible for the restoration of the relationship between God and his creatures lost in the original disobedience. For an older person today, then, to feel that he or she is less worthy, less acceptable, because of the deterioration of the body runs contrary to the fundamental message of the Christian faith.[21] Christians, recognizing that the human being is more than just body, should accept and value a person no matter what condition the body is in.

"Old and Full of Years"

Another contribution that the biblical tradition can make to a contemporary understanding of growing older stems from the Old Testament's view that dying "old and full of years" is a highly desirable goal, not a fate to be dreaded (as is so often heard today both from younger people—"I just hope I go quickly before I get too old"—and from older people—"Why didn't the Lord just take me before I got this way?"). One might liken the person "full of years" to a vessel full of liquid, that is, at its capacity: It can hold no more and has fulfilled its purpose by containing all that it was designed to hold. Similarly, to die "full of years" is to be satisfied, completed, indeed, "full-filled" in a most literal sense, having lived all the years one was intended to live. Thus the Old Testament can suggest of Abraham, for

149

example, that living longer would have had nothing more to offer him: To die "old and full of years" was the culmination of what God had planned for Abraham, and a death without fear was the natural conclusion of his fulfilled life. In short, in Hans Walter Wolff's apt words, "This is the death that man is *allowed* to die, not the one that he *has* to die."[22]

The imagery of dying "full of years" is especially helpful as one considers the problems of aging in today's society. Perhaps people are living *beyond* the point at which they are "full of years" in the sense of being filled to capacity and thus serving their purpose. Medical technology has become quite adept at keeping the bodily vessel around (and even in relatively good shape). Without an expansion of its capacity, of the purpose it exists to accomplish, however, the vessel cannot help ceasing to function as it should. Consequently it fails to be "full-filled." If contemporary society is going to continue to keep people alive and at the same time tell them that they no longer serve any useful purpose, then dying "in a good old age, old and full of years," in the biblical sense will be a thing of the past.

One concrete way in which older people can avoid the trap of an empty old age that modern society seems to have laid for them is to be more careful about the ways they choose to fill their later years. As chapter 1 showed, a major change in the situation of the elderly today is the length of time people survive after the traditional adult responsibilities of work and child-rearing are fulfilled. In contemporary American society this time is often a period of role and status attrition. One reason is that retirement often is filled with activities that have a legitimate place as occasional recreation but, as a steady diet, eventually lose their ability to make one feel worthwhile or to be viewed as such by others. Indeed, many typical retirement activities—golf, bridge, travel, and the like—illustrate that narcissistic values continue to thrive in the later years: All of these "pastimes" are quite *self*-centered, focusing attention upon oneself and doing little for anyone else. As this study has reiterated frequently, however, the Christian faith (not to mention the wisdom of the ages in almost all religious and philosophical traditions) emphatically teaches that attention to self is one of the least successful ways to find genuine fulfillment and satisfaction in life.

How much fuller might old age be if spent in some form of service to others? How much more purpose might be found for the sometimes seemingly endless time if the lost responsibilities of job and children are replaced, not exclusively with *self*-oriented recreational pastimes, but with activities that contribute to the welfare of *others*? Qoheleth observed long ago, "For everything there is a season, and a time for every matter under heaven" (Eccles. 3:1). One's later years well may be the season to answer more fully than ever before Christ's call to serve. As Hans Küng put it, the cross to which Christ calls his disciples is "the cross of everyday life," with all the "daily obligations, demands, claims, promises" that that implies. To serve others, to give of oneself, is surely one of the most obvious and legitimate ways of taking up one's cross and following Christ.

The elderly in fact possess in abundance one thing of great value which many younger people complain they never have enough of, namely, *time;* and it is precisely this time that, if left empty and purposeless, can be such a burden to the elderly. On the other hand, if put to use in ways that benefit others, the gift of free time can literally be a life-saver, by filling one's later years with purpose. The New Testament emphasis upon the continuing duties and responsibilities of older people, especially widows, may reflect a recognition of the importance of not letting one's later years be a period of empty and idle hours, if they are to constitute a "good old age." Certainly the truth of Jesus' teaching is apparent once more: It is as one turns away from

151

oneself and one's own needs and desires (i.e., "loses one's life") that one finds the meaning and fulfillment that seem to have been lost with advancing years (i.e., "saves one's life").

A Shift in Relationships Toward Mutual Responsibility

Indeed, for the Christian the entire discussion of the place and the role of the elderly in contemporary society, and of the obligations of younger people toward older, needs a radical reorientation. No longer can the issue be the *self*-fulfillment of one individual over against that of another but rather what the suffering of *each* for Christ's sake entails—the sacrifice of each amid the limitations and the suffering that are common to all human beings. Taken together with the cardinal belief that all Christians are united in and through Christ as members of his earthly body, the theology of the Cross advocated in this book leads to a major shift in the vocabulary used in discussing intergenerational relationships, a linguistic shift with significant impact if reflected in practice. Some of the more important of these shifts are from the *individual* to the *community* (or, to put it another equally valid way, from *self* to *other*); from *independence* to *interdependence*; from *self-fulfillment* to *sacrifice*; from *demand* to *gift*. It is crucially important that these shifts in perspective and emphasis take place on the part of *all* involved, older no less than younger.

Though a fuller consideration of the interrelationship between dependent and caregiver belongs to the next chapter, several comments about the responsibilities of older people are in order here. Just as the idea that virtue tends to reside in one socioeconomic group (the poor) has recently been called into question, so it must be stated that neither does virtue rest with one age group (the elderly). Though the obligations of the younger to the older are clear and inescapable, an obligation exists on the part of the elderly to continue to struggle against those feelings and desires that beset all human beings, such as self-centered-ness, lack of concern for others, and the failure to try to live for others.

For many elderly people today, however, coping with the losses of aging can take the form of making excessive demands upon younger people for attention, care, and support of various kinds (a practice, incidentally, that is probably as old as old age but may be exacerbated today by the movement for "elders' rights"). A theology of the Cross, however, would call upon older people to temper those demands, and one of their contributions to the relationship between the generations would be to sacrifice the satisfaction of some of the desires (and even perceived needs) that they feel the younger generation owes them.

Certainly no alleviation of human misery and no elevation of human hopes can occur if the different generations see their tasks as a competitive struggle rather than as a common enterprise. Sadly, as the elderly feel themselves increasingly pushed to the fringes of society (and beyond), they tend to adopt a "them against us" mentality. They may withdraw from contact with younger people (even into "elder ghettos"), refuse to support school bonds and other taxes perceived as benefitting only younger people, or in general decline to engage in the constructive kinds of interaction that are essential for the maintenance of any kind of community worthy of the name. As one older woman, very active in her community, remarked, "The old have an obligation to show the young that elderly people still have worthwhile contributions to make. That will not only help the older people to be treated better but also assist the younger to deal more positively and less fearfully with their own aging."

Unfortunately, as Dieter Hessel has pointed out, even "the church does little to challenge relatively complacent older people who assume that they have pretty much fulfilled their responsibilities, and can mark time before claiming the place reserved for them at the Messianic banquet."[23] Clergy (especially in retirement areas) often hear in response to a request for some service to the church, "I did that for forty years; I've put in my time already. Get one of these younger people with children to do it—they're the ones who'll benefit." As Hessel continues, though, "There is no age limit on God's expectation that persons contribute to the coming of the Kingdom, as we are reminded in the parable of the Great Feast (Lk. 14:15-24). The feast is ready but everyone (especially the retired?) seems to have an excuse." The biblical concept of a community founded on love—indeed, for Christians a community functioning as the earthly body of its Risen Lord, who has called all his followers to take up their own crosses as he once did—surely rejects making excuses for not participating in its work and activities, whatever one's age.

Age as a Teacher of Wisdom

Finally, chapter 1 discussed the shift in the modern world from industrial societies to information societies characterized by an emphasis on newly discovered knowledge based upon logic and reason rather than upon timeless wisdom gained from tradition and experience. Because of the detrimental impact of this "megashift" on attitudes toward aging and the elderly, further exploration is necessary at this point. In fact, the view of aging presented in this chapter can play a positive role in repairing some of the damage.

Until fairly recently in human history (as chapter 2 showed with regard to Hebrew society), the aged were highly valued for their wisdom, which was essentially the

154

accumulation of the experiences of their long years of life, supplemented by what they had learned through oral tradition from their elders. In addition to practical knowledge, such wisdom included the collective memories and stories that gave the particular society its identity and upon which the community based its existence. In short, the elderly were the "memory bank" for the culture, the repository for all the knowledge that really mattered in the community's life. In the progression from oral to written to printed to computerized transmission and storage of knowledge, however, the role of the individual as source of knowledge has virtually disappeared; people no longer are needed for this function because computers are available. It also is relevant that contemporary American society, secularized as it is, values much less the kinds of stories that always have been central to the wisdom that the elderly alone possessed.

Furthermore, in earlier times knowledge was useful for a much longer period than it is today: Generation A's experience and wisdom had considerable importance for Generation B and even for Generation C (and beyond), including real survival value. Individuals in Generation A, therefore, were essential for teaching those in B (and probably C) what they knew. Today knowledge is expanding so rapidly that yesterday's great discovery is archaic tomorrow. The most eagerly sought people are not those who have had the longest time to gain experience and master skills (the elderly) but those who have been trained most recently in the latest theories and techniques (the young).[24] In an information society, the time orientation thus turns from the past to the future, and value rests with those who can keep up with the flood of new information constantly being produced. As chapter 1 showed, the changes associated with the shift to an information society contribute to the devaluation of the elderly occasioned by role and status attrition.

Does this then mean that the traditional association of wisdom with age is no longer valid? Are the elderly really "odd man (and woman) out" in a world of exploding information that has passed them by? An important strain in biblical thought suggests one role that age still can play in human knowledge, namely, as teacher of a wisdom that is ultimately of greater importance than that which modern society values so highly. The Bible and the religious traditions that stem from it have long taught that human mortality is a great teacher of wisdom (at least if one will *recognize* one's mortality). The classic biblical example is Psalm 90, which stresses the brevity, "toil and trouble" of human life and then implores God, "So teach us to number our days that we may get a heart of wisdom" (v. 12). The theme is echoed throughout Ecclesiastes; Qoheleth stresses the "vanity of vanities" of all striving for the things that the world believes bring fulfillment (see especially 7:2; cf. 12:1-7, already considered in chapter 2).

In this tradition mortality is almost always associated with death, and the link is certainly not to be denied. No one knows for sure exactly when death will come, but it is certain to come to all, and when it comes it is absolutely final. An awareness of these characteristics of death can teach one a great deal about life. For example, radical uncertainty about the time of death can illuminate the value of each moment and the danger of procrastination based on the illusion that time for living is unlimited. The equality of death can expose the insignificance of the cultural standards by which human beings assign worth to themselves and one another; an understanding of our common fate reveals the artificiality of these distinctions and can heighten compassion. As Marcus Borg concludes, awareness of one's own death can help a person avoid losing his or her life in "procrastination, preoccupation, performance and postponement".[25]

If the association of death with mortality is obvious, it is equally undeniable that aging itself also well illustrates human mortality and therefore can be an excellent teacher of wisdom, too. In fact, in some ways aging might be a *better* teacher than death. That is, although the finality of death is unique and thus unparalleled in forcing one to confront one's mortality, it is also true that once one is dead, the wisdom gained from confronting death is of little use either to that person or to others. In addition, because of the death-denying nature of American society, most people will not think seriously about their own death until it is truly imminent, and many will not face up to it even then. So however good a teacher of wisdom death may be, it tends to arrive at the very end of the school day, if it even gets into the classroom at all.

On the other hand, *aging* as a teacher of wisdom, though lacking the finality of death, has the advantage, first, of gradually bringing one to the realization of personal mortality; second, of leaving one some time to apply and therefore benefit from that wisdom (which consists primarily in recognizing and accepting one's dependence upon others and ultimately upon God); and finally, of allowing one to serve as a model for others who might learn from one's example. If one can face up to one's aging and not deny it, if one can acknowledge how the losses of growing older are clear illustrations of human finitude and not try to hide them under a veneer of unrealistic optimism about old age's being the fulfillment of life, then aging can indeed help one to "get a heart of wisdom" and to move beyond the "vanity" of worldly standards of value.

Conclusion

Christians, informed both by their own heritage and by a realistic approach to the phenomenon of growing older, must move beyond the Pollyanna attitude toward aging current in Christian literature, a view that fails to take seriously the real losses that human beings suffer as they grow older. Such an alternative Christian approach will give a central place to the discipleship of the cross, recognizing that the cross Jesus Christ bids his followers to take up includes the ordinary, everyday sufferings of human life—including those associated with aging—that are borne as Jesus bore his sufferings. This understanding frees Christians to face the stark reality of old age, including the bad and the painful as well as the good and the uplifting. An honest recognition of the losses of aging, in fact, can lead one to accept one's utter dependence upon God, a necessity in the Christian scheme for restoring the relationship with God that has been disordered by human pride. Indeed, suffering and weakness not only are helpful reminders of the true human condition of limitation and dependence upon God but can also serve as an avenue for growing even closer to the Savior who, through his own weakness, suffering, and death on the cross for both young and old, showed the way to true fulfillment.

Furthermore, Christians can acknowledge the healthy concern for the body inherent in the Christian tradition and rightly lament the very real losses one experiences with age, without at the same time viewing the human being as only a body that must inevitably deteriorate. Such an understanding can lead, contrary to the prevailing view of contemporary American society, to the knowledge that human value depends not upon what one has or consumes but rather upon the fact that one is—a reflection of the biblical affirmation that God's standards are very different from those the world uses to judge personal worth. Helpful guidance for a Christian understanding of aging also comes from the biblical image of a timely death, arriving when one is "old and full of years."

In addition, a theology of the Cross, augmented by the scriptural teachings concerning love and community, suggests a radical reorientation of attitudes about the responsibilities of old and young, in the direction of greater mutuality and willingness to sacrifice. Older people in particular need to remember that Christ's call to serve others knows no time limit. In fact, one of the best ways the elderly can fill the time that would otherwise hang so heavy on their hands is precisely by seeking ways to help others. In the process, contemporary Americans are much more likely to discover "a good old age" for themselves.

Finally, despite the current view that devalues experience and "the wisdom of years" and maintains that the old have little to contribute to the world, the traditional understanding of age as a teacher of wisdom can still offer considerable insight into the development of the values that make for a humane society.

Much has been said now about ways that theological reflection upon biblical materials might help contemporary Christians as they struggle with the difficult and painful issues that aging raises. The last chapter will consider the matter of obligations to the elderly from the same perspective.

NOTES

1. The depth and the breadth of this response are illustrated by the appearance of the *Journal of Religion & Aging*, which began publication in 1984. As expressed in its statement of purpose, the journal has three basic goals: (1) "to inform religious professionals . . . about developments in the emerging field of religious gerontology"; (2) "to inform 'secular' professionals . . . who work with elderly people and their families within the context of religious institutions"; and (3) "to focus the attention of the traditional academic disciplines within religion on the phenomena of human aging."

2. Henri J. M. Nouwen and Walter J. Gaffney, *Aging: The Fulfillment of Life* (Garden City, N.Y.: Doubleday Image Books, 1974), pp. 19-20. The following

critique does not intend to suggest that such books cannot be helpful resources in a number of ways.

3. Alfons Deeken, *Growing Old, and How to Cope with It* (New York: Paulist Press, 1972), pp. 4-5.

4. Of course, such a view is not limited to *Christian* authors. As Abraham Heschel, the noted Jewish scholar, e.g., affirmed in his famous 1961 address to the White House Conference on Aging, "Old age is not a defeat but a victory, not a punishment, but a privilege. . . . Just to be is a blessing, just to live is holy." See "The Older Person and the Family in the Perspective of Jewish Tradition," in Carol LeFevre and Perry LeFevre, eds., *Aging and the Human Spirit: A Reader in Religion and Gerontology* (Chicago: Exploration Press, 1981), pp. 36, 44. Particular beliefs of Old Testament religion may inform Heschel's position; see chapter 2 above.

5. Indeed, a basic contradiction seems to exist in the current Christian approach to aging. On the one hand, the emphasis on the "golden opportunities" of aging criticized above leads many authors to urge that aging is not to be feared or resented but rather, as noted, to be anticipated and warmly greeted as a time of fulfillment, reflection, and peace. On the other hand, the classical Christian view of death as the final enemy suggests that it is to be fought and even avoided if possible (cf., e.g., Jesus in Gethsemane); and whatever else old age may be, it is unquestionably a sign that death cannot be far away.

6. See, e.g., Paul Ramsey, "The Indignity of 'Death with Dignity,' " *Hastings Center Studies* 2 (May 1974): 47-62; and Paul Santmire, "Nothing More Beautiful Than Death?" *Christian Century* (December 14, 1983): 1154-58.

7. For one way of viewing this point from a Christian perspective, see Stephen Sapp, ". . . As the Sparks Fly Upward," *Journal of Religion and Health* 16 (January 1977): 44-51, esp. 51.

8. Jn. 16:33*b*. The continuation of the verse, however, illustrates the legitimate Christian hope that exists *through* the cross: "but be of good cheer, I have overcome the world."

9. Martin Marty, *Context* (January 1, 1986): 4.

10. Hans Küng, *On Being a Christian,* trans. Edward Quinn (Garden City, N.Y.: Doubleday, 1976), p. 580; for simplicity, further page references to the book will be in the text.

11. Dietrich Bonhoeffer, *The Cost of Discipleship,* trans. R. H. Fuller, rev. and unabridged ed. (New York: Macmillan, 1959), p. 99. On p. 96 Bonhoeffer defines "discipleship" in terms very similar to those of Hans Küng quoted above: "Discipleship means adherence to the person of Jesus, and therefore submission to the law of Christ which is the law of the cross."

12. William F. May alludes to the point being made (and echoes the statements above about *daily* cross-bearing) in his provocative article, "Who Cares for the Elderly?" *Hastings Center Report* 12 (December 1982): 33: "To have to face the elderly daily would be too depressing. We prefer to remove from sight the decrepit (and the maimed, the disfigured, the infirm, and the retarded) because they inspire fear. They remind us of the impoverished side of ourselves. To address them in their needs would require us to acknowledge our own needs. It is preferable, even at great expense, to remove them from sight."

13. Mac Turnage and Anne Turnage, *Graceful Aging: Biblical Perspectives* (Atlanta: Presbyterian Office on Aging, 1984), p. 37.

14. William F. May, "Who Cares for the Elderly?" p. 32.

15. J. R. P. Sclater, "The Book of Psalms [1-41]: Exposition," in George A.

Buttrick et al., eds., *The Interpreter's Bible,* vol. 4 (Nashville: Abingdon Press, 1955), p. 127.

16. A particularly acute fear for many people today, with all the increased publicity about Alzheimer's disease and related dementias, is the loss of intellectual function, or at least of conscious control of one's own body.

17. For further explication of this point in a different context, see Stephen Sapp, *Sexuality, the Bible, and Science* (Philadelphia: Fortress Press, 1977), pp. 5-6, 117-18.

18. Harmon L. Smith, *Ethics and the New Medicine* (Nashville: Abingdon Press, 1970), p. 113.

19. Erich Fromm, *To Have or To Be?* (New York: Bantam Books, 1976), p. 15.

20. James Whitehead, "The Parish and Sacraments of Adulthood: Access to an Educational Future," *Listening: Journal of Religion and Culture* 12 (Spring 1977): 80; quoted in Evelyn Eaton Whitehead, "Religious Images of Aging: An Examination of Themes in Contemporary Christian Thought," in LeFevre and LeFevre, *Aging and the Human Spirit,* p. 64. The following quotation from Evelyn Whitehead is from the same page.

21. Furthermore, no indication appears anywhere in the Bible that the "image of God" is lost or reduced as one grows older (or for any other reason, for that matter). The value of this distinctive aspect of human nature, with all it means for one's relationship with God, thus remains intact regardless of what may be happening to one's physical being.

22. Hans Walter Wolff, *Anthropology of the Old Testament,* trans. Margaret Kohl (Philadelphia: Fortress Press, 1974), p. 112.

23. Dieter Hessel, "The Church's Response to Ageism," in Dieter Hessel, ed., *Empowering Ministry in an Ageist Society* (New York: The Program Agency, United Presbyterian Church, U.S.A., 1981), p. 67.

24. This attitude is reflected in the remark of a dentist when asked by a patient who was moving how to select a dentist in a new community: "Make sure you pick someone who has not been out of dental school more than ten years, preferably five. The practice of dentistry has changed so drastically in the past decade that you don't want someone with outdated ideas and techniques inside your mouth."

25. Marcus Borg, "Death as the Teacher of Wisdom," *Christian Century* (February 26, 1986): 204; the entire article is a good illustration of the traditional identification of mortality with death.

CONCERNING

OBLIGATIONS

TOWARD THE

ELDERLY

CHAPTER FIVE

The attitude that one holds toward aging undeniably affects one's attitude and behavior toward older people. Responsibilities in this area, therefore, will not be taken seriously if one fails to acknowledge one's own aging and to reach some sort of accommodation to that fact. The previous chapter offered some thoughts from biblical and theological perspectives to assist the Christian in dealing with his or her own aging. In this light, the obligations that one's faith sets forth in the area of interactions with the elderly are clearer and more meaningful.

Although the Bible presents a varied perspective on the meaning of growing older and how to cope with it, the responsibility of younger persons toward those who are older receives much more uniform treatment. This chapter will consider contemporary issues and problems in light of

162

what has been learned from the Bible about obligations toward the elderly.

Society's Response to the Elderly

Narcissism

The response of contemporary American society to the needs of the expanding elderly population is heavily influenced by what chapter 1 showed to be an increasingly prevalent attitude in the United States, namely, a self-centered, present-oriented approach to life that has been characterized as "narcissism." According to Christopher Lasch, modern society "has made the individual dependent on the state, the corporation, and other bureaucracies," with a consequent loss of the inner resources that yield genuine self-esteem. As a result, the narcissist must depend on others to impart a sense of worth to him or her through their admiration: The narcissist "needs to be admired for his beauty, charm, celebrity, or power—attributes that usually fade with time." Thus the "irrational terror of old age and death" in America today "is closely associated with the emergence of the narcissistic personality as the dominant type of personality structure."[1] Having lost the sense of historical continuity that allows one to take comfort in the carrying on of one's work by subsequent generations, the older narcissist can only resent the fact that younger people have come to possess the qualities in which she or he formerly found self-worth.

Contemporary society has managed to convince many of its citizens that "freedom," autonomy, and immediate gratification of personal desire are the most important values in life. The result is hardly beneficial, as Richard L. Rubenstein observes:

Possessive individualism has helped to make ours a society of universal otherhood rather than brotherhood. Such individualism mistakenly dichotomizes the individual and society. It also misconstrues self-realization as largely a private affair. It is congruent with free-enterprise capitalism and Social Darwinism. Unfortunately, it is incongruent with any theory of obligation that would make the fate of one's neighbor more than a prudential concern.[2]

Among the effects of this "possessive individualism," one of the most obvious and most detrimental has been the loss of a sense of responsibility for the impact that one's actions have upon others (and a consequent unwillingness to act differently if that would mean giving up something one wants for oneself). Along with this loss comes an inevitable erosion of the sense of community among people, because community requires a concern for the welfare of others (or at least of the "body" or group of which one is a member). Whatever the gain in individual freedom (and both Christianity and Judaism would raise serious questions about the legitimacy of freedom claimed in isolation from a responsibility to and *for* others), it does not seem that society as a whole stands improved by this shift.

In *Me: The Narcissistic American,* Aaron Stern points out that "narcissism and the capacity to love are directly related to each other. As one element increases, inevitably the other must decrease. The more narcissistic one is, the less he can love, and vice versa" (p. 13). As this chapter will demonstrate, Stern has gone directly to the heart of the matter, and Christianity will be seen to offer a distinctive solution.

A "Surplus Population"?

It is arguable that in the United States today the elderly are coming rapidly to be seen by many as a "surplus population." The phrase comes from a provocative and troublesome book by Richard L. Rubenstein, *The Age of Triage*, subtitled *Fear and Hope in an Overcrowded World*.[3] A surplus or "redundant" population is "one that for any reason can find no viable role in the society in which it is domiciled" (p. 1). With no role to play and consequently no standing in the society, such people do not receive the benefits of society that others do. Governments view them as sources of unrest and often try to control them or even to eliminate them entirely. The operative philosophy of such programs was concisely expressed in Kampuchea during the time that between one-quarter and one-half of the country's population was being killed: "There is nothing to gain by keeping them alive, nothing to lose by doing away with them" (p. 165).

Curiously, Rubenstein seldom mentions the elderly, being concerned primarily with the un- or underemployed and racial and ethnic minorities. Chapter 1 of this book, however, shows that many of America's older people fit the definition of a surplus population, especially given the attrition of role and status that accompanies growing older today. Most people in the United States, of course, will not easily tolerate the common solution to a surplus population discovered by Rubenstein because what it suggests runs so counter to values deeply ingrained in the American psyche (values, not incidentally, largely derived from the biblical tradition). Even firmly held values can change, however, and sometimes they are ignored in the face of perceived threats to a desired style of life. Rubenstein's balanced judgment thus is not to be lightly dismissed: "To date, America's method of coping with its surplus population has been more in keeping with what can justly be called a commitment to humanitarian values, but we do not know how the United States or any other large, relatively democratic country might act under conditions of pressing

165

material scarcity or an extended economic depression" (p. 23).

In this context, a comment must be made about current government policy described in chapter 1. The New Federalism has led to reduced government support of those seen as "non-contributors" to society (in an economic sense, at least), among whom many elderly are counted. That analysis in fact suggests that our country is not far from considering the elderly (certainly the "old old") to be a surplus population, as defined by Rubenstein. The assault upon some of the fundamental concepts of American society that this approach represents is well described by Rubenstein. After "insisting that *no human being ought to be considered surplus,*" he points out that though the law of the jungle may be survival of the fittest (which is what the philosophy of determining value on the basis of one's ability to produce amounts to), the jungle and the human community differ radically. In fact, the very purpose of human community is to provide both protection from "the ravages of the jungle" and a place where "decency and civility can govern the relations" among people. He then aptly asserts:

> When advocates of free-enterprise capitalism and Social Darwinism naturalize the human condition and claim that, as with all animals, the fundamental law of human existence is the survival of the fittest, they are in reality insisting that even in civil society the condition of mankind is one of the war of all against all.

Rubenstein concludes drily that this is hardly a conservative view but rather represents a radical departure from the values that have underlain American society since its founding (p. 228).[4]

After his careful examination and diagnosis, Rubenstein's prescription is significant. Arguing that in the past the social and demographic problems faced by modern society would be alleviated by mass migrations of people, Rubenstein claims that today's world precludes such a solution. Thus he asserts, "If we are to survive we have only the option of changing ourselves" (p. 33). The only way out, according to Rubenstein, is a complete reorganization of the economy to provide full employment as a permanent feature of American life. Because this program is hindered primarily by the philosophy of "possessive individualism" becoming dominant in American society, Rubenstein maintains, in a section entitled "The Need for a Religious Transformation," that "a purely secular, rationalistic approach to our social problems is unlikely to produce the collective altruism our situation demands" (p. 232, italicized in original). Reinforcing one of the main points of this book, he goes on to affirm, "Without religious values, the preferred solution to a social problem is likely to be the one involving fewest costs." Rubenstein concludes with words that bear remembering whenever the question of contemporary society's obligations to its elderly arises:

> The call for religious transformation is in reality a call to conversion, a call to change ourselves. Our preachers have rightly told us that we must be converted, that we must be born again. Unfortunately, what has been understood as conversion has all too often been devoid of the inclusive social component our times demand. In truth, we must be born again as men and women blessed with the capacity to care for each other here and now. (p. 240)

The relationship between Rubenstein's solution and the Christian message cannot be overlooked. The writings of Paul, for example, contain a great deal of instruction to the members of his churches concerning proper behavior in a number of areas. As Ernst Käsemann has observed, however, Paul's "ethical" exhortations always presuppose a prior "dogmatics." The believer's justification results in (or consists of) the claiming of that person's life by the lordship of Christ, and right behavior is the necessary implicate of salvation. Thus "Christian freedom and the new obedience manifest themselves only as the message of the gospel that God has reached out to the world and wills to have this confirmed and symbolically represented by the earthly conduct of the community."[5] Similarly, Hans Walter Wolff cites Micah 7:6 and comments specifically on the "chaotic difficulties" between generations that "seem inescapable where men—whether the older or the younger generation—see themselves as the final court of appeal and put themselves in the place of God, instead of living with the goodness of his word." The solution that he suggests echoes Käsemann's view: "With the entry of Jesus Christ into human history and the offer of unconditional reconciliation which it means, every dissension is to be seen as at most the penultimate phase in the relationship of generations; and it is as such that it should be treated."[6]

Rubenstein's solution, despite his calling it a "religious" transformation, comes from a basically humanistic perspective and thus lacks what all such approaches lack, namely, some inner dynamic that will allow people to do what they may know they should do but find themselves unable to do on their own. Christianity possesses precisely this power, and it is time now to discover some of the aspects of the Christian faith that make it so relevant to this discussion.

A Christian Response to the Elderly

At the heart of any community, and especially characteristic of those growing out of the biblical tradition, is the "sustaining story" of the community that gives it identity and character. Stanley Hauerwas and Richard Bondi point out that abandoning or challenging this story is called, in theological terms, "sin[,] as we literally forget what we are about as people who have been created by a God who sets our way." The theological ethicist's task is to remind the community of its sustaining story and to increase understanding of the moral skills that the story offers to those who follow it. Hauerwas and Bondi conclude, "Theology, therefore, is the attempt to keep us faithful to the character (the story and skills) of our community lest we forget who and why we are. It charges the imagination by helping us to notice those images that provide convictions that will truthfully form our existence."[7]

This book contends that the values regarding obligations to the elderly that are being increasingly demonstrated in American society threaten to lead Christians into a wholesale forgetting of "who and why" Christians are. As Hauerwas and Bondi observe, "If we have no convictions our culture will provide them for us, and if our convictions are poorly understood or weakly held the cultural configuration will override them. It is only by a continual recourse to the sources of the strength of our convictions that we can articulate and hold them in this world."[8]

Based on a reexamination of some of the basic sources for the Christian sustaining story, the preceding chapter suggested an alternative view of aging: Over against the attitude toward growing older prevalent in current Christian writing on the subject—a tendency toward too positive an assessment of the "joys of aging"—a more honest recognition of the losses associated with growing older, especially when viewed in light of a theology of the Cross, is preferable. Concerning obligations toward the elderly, this chapter recalls those who claim to have their character and identity formed by the sustaining story of Christianity to the clear message of that story with regard to caring for the elderly in a rapidly changing society.

As with most ethical issues, Christians of good conscience can differ, even vehemently, on matters pertaining to aging and obligations toward the elderly. Situations do vary, and the variables render insistence upon an absolute application of any point of view foolish. The position taken below therefore cannot be applied legalistically without regard for particular circumstances. In theory, the viewpoint of this chapter appears to be more in line with the sustaining story of the biblical tradition than is the prevailing attitude of contemporary American society; in practice, Christians must weigh the facts of their unique situations and act in the way that their understandings of the sustaining story leads them.

What are some of the major aspects of the sustaining story that has given Christians their character, identity, and moral direction for almost two thousand years? Which ones must be made "present in mind" if contemporary Christians are to act in ways that faithfully express who and why they are?

Love

Among many aspects of the sustaining story of Christianity that have direct relevance to the question of treatment of the elderly, one stands out from the earlier survey of biblical/theological material, namely, the love that Jesus demonstrated and commanded his followers to show to others. In fact, the love at the heart of the Christian story contrasts sharply with the narcissism so prevalent today because, as chapter 3 pointed out, it demands that Christians be servants to their fellows. Consideration of one further New Testament passage will give a better understanding of the importance of this distinction.

Mark 12:28-34 presents an important teaching of Jesus concerning the nature of love and its role in human life. In response to a question about the greatest commandment, Jesus quoted two Old Testament texts. The first quotation has to do with loving God with every aspect of one's personality, and the second—of interest here—is, "You shall love your neighbor as yourself" (v. 31). The judgment of virtually every commentator on human nature who has ever considered the matter is that genuine love of others is impossible unless one feels positively toward oneself. Jesus knew this, along with the fact that human beings are innately inclined to value themselves, and thus he used love of self as a model for the type of love that one should have for one's neighbor, that is, a virtually automatic, uncalculating regard for the other's welfare.

Love of others, of course, is important not only for the person doing the loving but also for the one receiving the love. In the case of the elderly, a lack of being loved sets up a vicious circle: If older people were not made to feel unloved, useless, unwanted, and resented—a bothersome burden with nothing worthwhile to contribute—they would not have to be so insecure, so demanding, so fearful about their place in the scheme of things, so concerned about the amount and the quality of time and attention they are getting. One of the major difficulties in this area is thus a kind of self-fulfilling prophecy: Society has decided that older people have little or nothing to contribute, and older people have adopted that expectation. The message that the elderly constantly receive is illustrated by the answer of a boy to a test question about what George Washington would think of the United Nations if he were still alive: "If he were alive today, he would be so extremely old that his opinions on any subject would be worthless." Victoria Bumagin and Kathryn Hirn thus conclude, "The assumption that not much can be expected of the elderly makes it more difficult for the elderly to expect very much of themselves."[9]

Not being loved and valued, then, can lead the elderly to a loss of the self-esteem necessary for human beings to function in a healthy manner. This leads to the next step in

171

the vicious circle, an attempt to regain the lost self-esteem through various undesirable means. One of the most common ways to do this is to turn inward and become concerned primarily, if not exclusively, with one's own interests. The attitude that contemporary society holds about the aged thus contributes significantly to some of the traits that people find distasteful in many older people (and that makes them more difficult to love in the way that Jesus intended), namely, self-concern, selfishness, unwillingness to give of themselves for the sake of others, in short, a failure to love others and to be a contributing part of the community. Robert Butler points to the same root cause that was suggested in Jesus' teaching: "Ageism, like all prejudices, influences the self view and behavior of its victims. The elderly tend to adopt negative definitions of themselves and to perpetuate the very stereotypes directed against them, thereby reinforcing society's beliefs."[10] Holding different attitudes about the elderly would go far toward relieving this particular problem, as would a more realistic, healthier view of one's own aging. In particular, a return to the respect for the elderly so central to the biblical view would help older people retain their self-respect.

A final comment is appropriate here about one suggested solution to the "problem" of the elderly: A widely discussed characteristic of modern society is the almost unquestioned belief that virtually any problem can be solved by the development of better technology. Although recent events may have caused a reduction of public expressions of this belief, it is so deeply ingrained in the American psyche as to be practically invincible, and for many it applies to the issues of aging and the elderly as much as to fuel and food shortages (cf., e.g., the prolongevity advocates mentioned in chapter 1). Here, however, the hope of a "technological fix" is especially misplaced, not only because many of the "problems" of aging are not particularly amenable to technological solution but also, and more significantly, because without an underlying change of heart such remedies will not address the real issue. John LaFarge, S.J., makes the point with a simple, yet telling, illustration: Hearing aids are grand because they enable the deaf person to rejoin society, from which she or he has been cut off. But what good is being able to hear if no one wants to talk with an older person, or if the only conversation available is hostile and critical? He concludes that like other machines, a hearing aid is "an aid to human intercourse, but only the loving will of your fellow human being can *create* the acceptable interchange of knowledge, emotion, and ideas."[11]

Community

A second cardinal element in the sustaining story of Christianity, and one that is closely related to the Christian view of love, is the concept of community, the importance of which is indisputable in biblical thought. The notion of the "covenant people" that is at the heart of ancient Israel's faith clearly expresses the centrality of community, as do Jesus' proclamation of the future yet present "Kingdom of God" and Paul's great image of the church as the earthly body of Christ. Indeed, after a careful search for a normative biblical theme upon which to base her Christian ethics, Lisa Sowle Cahill finally decides that "community" is what she is seeking: "New Testament ethics is thoroughly communal. . . . The moral life . . . is to be judged by a *communal criterion.* . . . The horizon against which *all* moral activity is to be evaluated is the communal life as body of Christ in the world."[12]

Obviously, the Bible offers a number of insights pertinent to this central doctrine. For example, as chapter 2 showed, Hebrew religion recognized in some of its earliest writings

173

that community is essential for truly human existence. In the creation stories, God is depicted as virtually saying, "I could make humans any number of ways, but I choose to make them so that they need other humans." Continuing this theme, the concern for the needy expressed throughout the Old Testament had a communal basis rooted in religion: Yahweh was linked in community with his people by the covenant, and the people were thus united through their relationship with him and modeled their interactions with one another on the *chesed* (faithful love) that he demonstrated toward them. Furthermore, the individual existed only as part of a community, and the issue for Old Testament thought was not, as for contemporary society, to create a community out of many widely differing individuals, but instead to discover within the fundamental given of community a place for individuals with autonomy and personal responsibility. This perspective represents a sharp divergence from the narcissistic attitude that has come to dominate Western society, in which the individual is the unquestionable given, with a right to self-determination and self-fulfillment limited only by similar and competing rights of others; the community in this contemporary view exists only to serve the individual.

Given the importance of community in Old Testament thought, it is significant that older people remained such integral, contributing, and valued members of Israelite society. Old age, even with the frank acknowledgment of the losses accompanying it, was no reason to deny a person membership and participation in the community. Although certain categories of individuals were excluded from the community, there is no indication that age was ever used as a criterion for such exclusion. Indeed, the important position of the elders suggests that far from disqualifying a person from a position of power and prestige within the community, advanced age was seen as imparting certain qualities, such as wisdom and insight, that made one especially suited for leadership and thus gave one a *central* place in the community. Furthermore, given that the family was the very heart of the larger community, the emphasis upon the care of elderly parents indicates that in the view of the covenant people, their God meant for older people not only to remain within the community but also to receive its benefits, just as the community earlier had received benefits from them. The biblical understanding of community clearly precludes any view of the elderly as a surplus population.

In the New Testament the Christian finds rich material to supplement the Old Testament message. For Christians the notion of community goes considerably beyond the Old Testament concept of the covenant people of Yahweh, allowing greater emphasis to be placed on the autonomy and worth of the individual (though not nearly so much emphasis as expressed by a great deal of Christian theology). The most important New Testament source is surely Paul, and he gives explicit, vivid expression to the depth and the breadth of the Christian concept of community in two important teachings.

The first is the imagery of the church as Christ's earthly body, which Paul uses in 1 Corinthians 12 to describe the proper relationship among members of the church. Two points about Paul's imagery of the church as a body are of interest to this study. First, if Christians relate to one another as members of a body, then the injury or suffering of one member has an effect on all the others, and they are well advised to do what they can to alleviate the pain. Second, because of this organic union, which implicates all members of the body in the suffering (and pleasure) of each member (v. 26), the "more presentable" members have no grounds for looking down on the "less honorable" members or for neglecting their welfare. Conversely, the "weaker" members also should not feel that they have no role to play in the life of the body because "God has so composed the body, giving the greater honor to the inferior part, that there may be no discord in the body, but that the members may have the same care for one another" (vv. 24-25). In contemporary American society (and the church is not to be excluded), the young too often look upon the old as weaker and inferior members of the body (politic or ecclesial), and the aged too readily accept this judgment. Recognition of the mutuality of need and support in Paul's image of community is important in order to counteract this prevalent tendency.

A second and equally significant expression of Paul's view of the nature of Christian community is his well-known statement of Christian oneness in Galatians 3:27-28: "For as many of you as were baptized into Christ have put on Christ. There is neither Jew nor Greek, there is neither slave nor free, there is neither male nor female; for you are all one in Christ Jesus" (cf. Col. 3:10-11). Given the current situation, it is legitimate to add to the apostle's affirmation, "there is neither young nor old," because *that* pairing is rapidly taking on the overtones of mutual fear and animosity, inequality, and divisiveness that the three archetypal distinctions addressed by Paul had in his day.

The theological reason behind Paul's position is significant. Romans 3:22*b*-24 is as succinct a statement of his logic as can be found: "For there is no distinction; since all have sinned and fall short of the glory of God, they are justified by his grace as a gift, through the redemption which is in Christ Jesus." No one therefore has any claim to superiority over anyone else—and certainly not on the basis of something so superficial as social class, gender, or age—when everyone stands on common ground as those who have been redeemed from their sin by the death of Jesus Christ. Paul thus adds a distinctively Christian ingredient to the equality of all human beings implicit in their creation "in the image of God": Now all are equal not only because they reflect God's likeness in some way; they are on common ground also as sinners whose only claim to righteousness is through the atoning work of Jesus Christ. Just as creation in God's image imputes worth to all human beings, so also (and even more so) does the fact that the Son of God died for them.

An important point concerning the Christian approach to the elderly arises from this consideration of community. Because of the nature of Christian community (stemming as it does from each believer's union with the risen Christ, the "head" of the community of believers), those who make up the "members" of the "body" are in organic union with one another, just as the parts of a human body are inextricably interrelated. And just as it is in the interests of the body (and therefore of each individual member of it) to have each member (and therefore the body as a whole) as healthy as possible, so those united through love in the Christian community should strive to make each member as "healthy" and strong as possible in every way. Surely, then, the community of believers should be a place within which all people remain valued members of the body.

Of course, gifts and talents differ (*throughout* lifetimes, it should be noted, not just when one gets older; cf. 1 Cor. 12:4-11), and some members of the community will need greater expressions of love in the form of service than will others. As is made clear in 1 Corinthians 13 and elsewhere, however, Christian love does not permit the patronizing of those whom one serves but rather demands their upbuilding. Christians therefore must be careful not merely to provide services *for* the elderly but to try to serve *with* them in meeting God's call for justice and compassion for all his creatures. Through this concrete expression of respect for the continuing value of the older person, the one served retains a sense of personal worth and is encouraged to help

177

herself or himself as well as others. Perhaps the key is to see the elderly as the Bible suggests God does, not as members of the class of "people over sixty-five," but as *individuals* within the community who are important and whose true well-being is essential for the health of the community. One then serves by asking always what is truly best for the individual, not what is most convenient, efficient, or cost-effective for the service provider.

In adopting this attitude, the Christian is only emulating the approach that Jesus is reported in the Gospels to have used in his interactions with people young and old. He always respected their independence and never overrode their freedom to live their own lives (cf., e.g., the rich young man in Mk. 10:17-22 and Nicodemus in Jn. 3:1-21). A similar attitude toward providing care for the elderly is strongly urged by virtually all authorities in the field today. As Dianne Springer and Timothy Brubaker put it, "It is our belief that a caregiver's objective should be to provide an environment where a 'dependent' older person is encouraged to move to his or her greatest possible degree of independency in as many facets of life as possible."[13] That advice hardly differs from what the Christian's goal should be in every interaction with all people, regardless of age.

It is appropriate in this context to remember that the elderly decline gradually and thus should not have all responsibility suddenly removed from them. The significant difference between "parental" duty and "filial" duty must be kept in mind. Although aging parents may require their adult children's assistance, the children must continue to consider their parents adults for the parents' sake as well as for the children's. Seeing responsibilities to one's parents in the same light as duties toward one's children tends to cause the elderly parents to be treated as if they were children. Indeed, is not one of the major problems in interacting appropriately with the elderly the all too

178

tempting tendency to reduce them to a level of childish dependence, denying them their rightful place in the community to which they have contributed for decades?

Obligations to Parents and Other Elderly Persons

Although the state has taken upon itself many of the responsibilities once met by families (thus encouraging the trend away from their assuming such responsibility), this state aid is now decreasing. Where will help to fill the void be found? Research reported in chapter 1 has demonstrated that families are unquestionably the primary source of assistance to the needy elderly, and it is hard to argue that a better solution to the need exists. Government, social service agencies, even the churches have not shown a particular ability (or willingness) to respond to the needs of the dependent elderly in a way that should satisfy any humane person, much less a Christian committed to the basic biblical principles for human relationships. From whatever perspective one considers the issue (with the possible exception of the freedom of the younger family members to satisfy all their own desires), the family *can* provide the best setting for an elderly person's final, dependent years. Whether it *will* do so or not is the issue today.

What guidance, then, can Christianity provide in addressing this vexing question? The command to *love* one's neighbor as oneself—a love that manifests itself in a willingness to be a servant to others—lies at the heart of the Christian sustaining story. This love underlies and empowers the key concept of *community*, which emphasizes the mutuality of the various "members" of the body, leading to the demand that each take a vital interest in the welfare of all. These two elements give rise to a clear and unequivocal affirmation: *Adult children have a responsibility for the care of their elderly parents.*

This claim finds explicit scriptural support in the fifth commandment of the Decalogue: "Honor your father and your mother, that your days may be long in the land which the Lord your God gives you" (Ex. 20:12). Chapter 2 presented a detailed analysis of this central statement. Merely quoting Rolf Knierim's apt summary of the intention of the commandment will recall the major findings of that examination: "The command to honor father and mother must be understood holistically, in the sense of taking care of, supporting, protecting, and respecting parents as long as they live. It reflects a genuine form of social security in which the old parents remained part of their families, with dignity and material security."[14]

The Christian, of course, is not limited to the teachings of the Old Testament—especially the Law—and finds further revelation of God's will in the New Testament. Such is the case with this matter as well, but the additional information only strengthens and supports the message of the fifth commandment. As chapter 3 showed, Jesus is depicted as expressing concern about older parents in at least two places. First, the controversy with the Pharisees about the Corban vow (Mk. 7:1-23) demonstrates the evangelist's perception of how seriously Jesus took the divinely ordered care of parents. In an insightful anticipation of the situation in America today (discussed at the beginning of this chapter), Jesus suggested that such a shirking of responsibilities reflects the desire to follow one's *own* will rather than God's (at least the Pharisees could claim that what they were advocating in some way honored *God*).

Second, Jesus' provision of care for his mother even as he hung dying on the cross (Jn. 19:26-27) vividly depicts his concern for the needs of parents who cannot provide for themselves. Given this example of Jesus' action, especially under the circumstances, to imagine that those who claim to follow Jesus today can find justification for failing to provide for their parents in need is indeed difficult.

In addition to these examples from the Gospels, the most explicit statement of the New Testament regarding obligations toward elderly parents concerns the care of widows. This matter received attention in chapter 3; here it is sufficient to reiterate that the early church, interpreting the impact of the love of Jesus Christ upon the lives of those who follow him and reflecting the communal nature of the body of believers, left little room for neglecting the responsibility of children (and even grandchildren) to care for elderly parents (at least widows) who could no longer provide for themselves. The church certainly has an obligation to help when no other aid is available, but the unmistakable message is that where family members exist, they are to be the primary source of support.

Individual Responsibility

The apparently unequivocal demand of Scripture to provide for the needs of one's elderly parents will not be received happily by many Christians today. After all, general calls to community and love lend themselves to all sorts of "safe" commitments; a specific demand to provide for the care of elderly parents brings the obligation much closer to home, perhaps too close. As Father Zossima in Dostoevsky's *The Brothers Karamazov* so insightfully asserted, "The more I love humanity in general, the less I love man in particular. . . . One can love one's neighbors in the abstract, or even at a distance, but at close quarters it's almost impossible."[15]

Given the implications of the central elements of the Christian sustaining story discussed above, the issue concerning obligations to elderly parents appears to be one not so much of determining what is right but of acknowledging that many people simply do not *want* to do it. Daniel Callahan puts the matter into sharp focus:

> The issue, as it presents itself, may be less one of trying to discover the grounds of obligation that would require a response than one of trying to find grounds for ignoring a demand that so patently assaults the sensibilities. It is not so much "must I?" as it is "how can I not?"[16]

The "patency" of the demand is far from universally granted, however, and questions—raised both by theory and by action—abound concerning its validity in the world of a twentieth-century information society beset with all the changes and the stresses outlined in chapter 1. Perhaps there really was a time when everything was significantly simpler, when obligations were more clearly recognized and more easily fulfilled, and when the elderly were not a "problem" but a blessing. It is obvious, however, that such a time is past for modern Americans. Nonetheless, what this book has said up to this point demonstrates that at least for Christians the grounds of obligation are quite clear, and the demand also seems rather patent. Recalling several of the biblical themes considered earlier, Gibson Winter aptly concludes: "We are continually confronted in this life with decisions for and against our parents, friends, and enemies. These decisions are the inescapable meetings with God. In turning against our responsibilities to others, we turn against God who binds us to them in mutual love."[17]

The earlier discussion of Christian love contributes a much needed element here: Precisely because it is *other*-directed and thus runs counter to the innate human tendency to put self first, to love as Christ demands is to confront the cross once again. Only as one loses oneself in service to others does one find the self that God intends each of his creatures to be. Fulfilling what Christianity teaches are one's obligations to the elderly, and especially to

182

one's older parents, unquestionably will interfere with one's freedom, with one's ability to do and to have what one wants when one wants, in fact with one's opportunities to find "*self*-fulfillment." As the last chapter demonstrated, however, at the heart of the Christian faith properly interpreted lies the cross and its demands for self-sacrifice. Thus, just as aging itself may be understood best in light of a theology of the Cross, so one's obligations toward the elderly also can find needed illumination from the same source.

Indeed, one must ask whether caring for an elderly parent is any more difficult, any more of a self-sacrifice, than the other sacrifices Christians are called to make for the sake of their Lord (whose own sacrifice for the sake of all was incomparable). Certainly the losses that adult children are going to suffer in committing themselves to the care of an older parent may be quite significant, but do they really compare to "laying down one's life" or even to "selling all that one has"? In short, *is the problem really one of not knowing what is right or best for the elderly, or is it simply the age-old proclivity to put one's own desires before the needs of others?*

"The world," of course, will call such an approach foolishness and archaic self-flagellation (recall the remarks quoted at the beginning and end of chapter 1), and by the world's standards such a judgment will be correct. In a narcissistic society the prospect of assuming the awesome responsibility of caring for an elderly person (or even of providing for his or her care) runs contrary to all that one is taught about the goal of life.

The Christian, however, cannot accommodate to society or adopt society's standards without ceasing to be her- or himself. As pointed out earlier, God's standards are different from the world's, and the Christian is called upon to "body forth" those standards even in opposition to the world. Such behavior will often cause suffering, not only because God's demands go against the human tendency to serve oneself rather than others but also because they make the person who tries to follow them look "different" in the eyes of the "wise" and the "strong." Few people find that enjoyable. Christians, however, are the eschatological community called to serve, not to be served, and to be an example of the kind of community all human beings could have if they would accept God's gracious gift through Jesus Christ. This calling rules out seeking every possibility to avoid or to rationalize the heavy demand of Christ to love others as he first loved everyone—a love that was willing to give up even life for the sake of others. Certainly the demands of Christ apply to the Christian's obligations toward the elderly, especially one's own aged parents, and the complaint of interference with one's self-fulfillment and personal desires just does not seem to carry a great deal of weight when viewed in the light of the cross.

DIRECT CARE   As chapter 1 showed, both older people and their adult children want the elderly to live independently if possible. Furthermore, at any given time only around 5 percent of the elderly in this country are in institutions (though they have a one in four chance of being institutionalized at some point before their death). The biblical emphasis on the value of the individual, manifesting itself in this case in a sensitivity to the need for autonomous living and decision-making, argues for striving diligently to enable the elderly to live independently for as long they can. Without doubt this is by far the best situation for all concerned, provided of course that the older person really is capable of functioning adequately on his or her own; even in this case, though, younger members of the family are certainly not without responsibilities.

What of the situation, however, when elderly parents need substantial assistance to live safely or especially when they no longer can live alone? The purpose of this section is not to give specific instructions for every possible situation but to offer a principle upon which to base decisions about how to fulfill one's obligations to one's parents.[18]

Ideally, it appears that the obligation of adult children to their dependent elderly parents is best met by direct care, which usually would involve coresidence. The standard to use in deciding whether this is the proper approach is quite simple: If the primary reason for not wanting to assume the care of a dependent parent is that such care impinges on the caregiver's "freedom," as understood by contemporary narcissistic society, the Christian view of love would have to consider such a reason invalid. Self-sacrifice has been shown to be essential to the Christian's vocation, and this fact colors any consideration of one's *ability* to care for an aged parent. That is, the claim that one is not able to care for a parent must not rest on the inconvenience that might be caused, including the fact that expenses incurred prevent one from doing some things one might want.

Furthermore, even though many adult children may lament their filial responsibility because their elderly parents become rather unpleasant individuals—emotionally and physically—as they grow older, the Christian gospel does not exempt even the unlovely and unlovable from those whom the follower of Jesus is commanded to love. In fact, it appears that these are *precisely* the ones for whom Christians *are* commanded to care. As Karl Barth put it so forcefully, "On the basis of the eternal will of God we have to think of *every human being,* even the oddest, most villainous or miserable, as one to whom Jesus Christ is Brother and God is Father; and we have to deal with him on this assumption."[19] Paul Ramsey, discussing the parable of the Good Samaritan, amplifies the point by saying that Christian love is unique among ethical standpoints "because it alone begins with neighborly love and not with *discriminating between worthy and unworthy people* according to the *qualities they possess.*"[20]

The natural human tendency is to do things for those one finds attractive, especially those who can give something in return. Christ's command, however, is to do for the "least of these" (Mt. 25:40), and the elderly are one of the best examples of what Jesus meant here. Perhaps God is giving those in the world today who normally do not encounter "the least" a chance to do what they should by providing so many elderly people, who may be more difficult to avoid than other needy people.

It is important to note that the motivation for caring for an aged parent is not a sterile sense of obligation—a wooden rehearsal of what one has been told one *should* do—but an active willingness to follow one's Lord in sacrificial love for the benefit of others, in this case someone to whom one is bound by many ties. First Samuel 16:7 speaks for the biblical tradition in pointing out that the internal motivation and not merely the form of the external act is determinative: "Man looks on the outward appearance, but the Lord looks on the heart" (cf. Mt. 15:17-20; Lk. 6:45). Certainly the attitude of the caregiver, and therefore in all likelihood the quality of care, will be influenced greatly by the reason one undertakes and continues the responsibility (acknowledging, as the previous chapter advocated, the difficulties inherent in aging).

INDIRECT CARE   The Christian's obligation to elderly parents ideally would be fulfilled best by direct care. The ideal situation regarding marriage, of course, is that no marriage end in divorce; and ideally in life in general, the righteous should always succeed and the unrighteous fail. Human life is obviously far from ideal. At some point, therefore, (or in some situations, from the outset) direct care of an elderly parent may not be best (e.g., if the caregiver is her- or himself too infirm or too obligated to young children to be able to provide proper care, or if the elder has reached a point of physical and mental deterioration that again precludes adequate home care). In this situation the same standard applies. If one wants to care for or to continue caring for the person out of a sense of pride, of "living up to one's duties" without regard for what is really best for all involved, then the Christian standard of selfless love would have to question such motives. In this case wanting to care for an elderly parent would be just as wrong as not wanting to because of the inconvenience and the infringement of one's autonomy.

This book has suggested that the answer to the narcissism prevalent in modern American society is love, and that for Christians that love is always other-directed, not self-serving. In situations such as the one under consideration here, it may be particularly difficult to make the distinction between the two. That is, what may appear to be self-sacrifice (insistence upon caring for an aged parent) in fact can turn out to be merely another manifestation of pride, a refusal to acknowledge one's limits and to turn to others for help, out of the fear of appearing weak and dependent. One cannot give in to narcissistic tendencies by insisting upon caring for an infirm parent when it is not really in the *parent's* best interests to do so. Here the love that Christians are called to display would demand forgoing one's own desires in favor of the genuine well-being of the other and asking appropriate people and institutions in the community to become involved in the care of the parent.

The institution that most readily comes to mind in this context is the church. In addition to its responsibility to prepare its members better for their own aging (along the lines suggested in chapter 4), the church should help those facing painful decisions about care of the elderly to understand the issues just discussed. As the body of believers of which both the aged person and the caregiver(s) are a part, the church must do a better job of assisting the increasing number of people who will be struggling with this problem in the years ahead.

Corporate Responsibility

Given the data presented in chapter 1 concerning the extent of interaction between the elderly and their families, one is tempted to say merely that a continuation of what is already happening is sufficient. Other factors cited in the same chapter, however, raise a concern that the sense of mutual responsibility that has characterized families in societies influenced by the biblical tradition may be waning, a trend that bodes ill for the care of the elderly in the future. In addition, then, to helping to respond to the question of the obligations of individuals to their elderly parents, the Christian sustaining story also has something to say to the church and to society in general.

After a period of attack upon the institution of the family from a number of quarters, most serious social observers are recognizing once again the family's essential role in creating and maintaining a civilized culture. In a democratic society a healthy family is the only really viable vehicle for transmitting values and producing mature citizens with positive self-identities. Loving human beings most often find their origin in the nurturing circle of a loving family. Similarly, at the other end of life the family might be the only real answer to the massive problems facing this country in the next century when the full impact of the demographic shift outlined in chapter 1 is felt. If the family, then, is a key factor in assuring the *future* quality of care of the elderly that a humane society surely desires, a logical conclusion follows: The mounting of a major effort is needed *now* to

188

strengthen families and even to train children from the outset to value and to care for parents.

Consider the conclusion of Victor G. Cicirelli after a thorough review of relevant research about the relationship between adult children and their elderly parents: "The amount of interaction . . . does depend on the closeness of the affectional bond, although other factors may also have an effect (duty, parent dependency, other responsibilities). This indicates that attachment to the parent motivates contact with the parent to some degree throughout the life of the parent."[21] Obviously if the "affectional bond" between parent and child is weakened or lacking altogether, the major motivation for care of the parents in their later years is lost.

One must ask, then, what contemporary society is doing to the future situation of the elderly by permitting the widely noted breakdown of the family. Children are being produced whose upbringing—marked by early and constant baby-sitters and day care, frequently absent parents who are preoccupied and harried (and often exhausted) when present, and a society that teaches them that immediate satisfaction of their personal desires is the goal of life—seems virtually designed to lead to a greatly reduced affectional bond with their parents, and this at a time when the number of elderly people is rising dramatically and the number of offspring to assume their care has decreased markedly.[22]

A serious effort to strengthen the family would necessarily involve focusing on the quality of the marriages that are at the heart of healthy families,[23] and several important side benefits might accrue from this initiative. For example, as chapter 1 suggested, divorce complicates the situation of the elderly for several reasons, not least of which is that older married partners tend to care for and to sustain one another, and divorce obviously eliminates such support. The increased number of women in the work force also significantly decreases the availability of care for elderly parents, but strong marriages that are marked by a sense of equality between the partners can lead to greater sharing of elder-care responsibilities, just as such an attitude has led recently to more participation by both parents in child care.

This discussion prompts an interesting thought: How obligated will children of the increasing number of nonmarital relationships feel toward parents who themselves were not committed enough to each other to formalize their relationship? Such a situation (implicitly, and often explicitly, based on the claim that "what society ' thinks and says doesn't matter") hardly seems the best teacher of the depth of familial commitment and obligation needed to assure the care of elderly parents.

One factor that would help strengthen the family is a reconceptualization of the nature of the family itself, to acknowledge more realistically the role of the elderly in modern society. Chapter 1 demonstrated that just as changes in the family have had an impact upon aging and the elderly, so changes in aging have had an effect upon the family. The time may have come, in the words of Matilda White Riley, to "think of a family less as the members of one household with incidental linkages to kin in other households and more as a continuing interplay among intertwined lives within the entire changing kinship structure."[24] Reflected here is the recognition that there *are* relationships among the generations that cannot be merely wished away because they may be inconvenient or troublesome and that such relationships can provide the arena for growth, true fulfillment, and maturation on the part of all who are involved in them. Thus instead of considering the one-generation nuclear family to be the normative structure, to which the older generation(s) must be seen as an (often bothersome and unwanted) *addition,* one would see the older members of the family as a part (in fact, the origin) of the "continuing interplay among intertwined lives."

This reconceptualization of the family brings to mind once again the biblical emphasis upon community, especially the Old Testament notion of "corporate personality" and the New Testament concept of "the body of Christ." To consider the family according to this model, instead of as a collection of individuals who merely use each other for personal need-satisfaction, would heighten the awareness that what one individual does affects the well-being of the entire family and, conversely, what the family as a group does obviously affects each member.

If viewed in this way, some of the more painful conflicts that inevitably arise in decisions about the care of elderly family members might appear in a new light. For instance, what is currently seen by many as competition between the needs of elderly parents and dependent children could be considered more "somatically," as one might think of ways to keep various parts of the body warm when one is underclad on a cold day. The view of family advocated here would contribute to the new vocabulary of interaction on the part of both younger and older members suggested in the last chapter, with "demand" replaced by "gift," "self-ful-fillment" by "sacrifice," and "independence" by "interdc-pendence." When one has the flu, one does not understand alleviating the headache to be in competition with settling the upset stomach; rather, the *overall* health of the body, which can be achieved only by attention to the welfare of *all* the members, is the goal. Furthermore, one is willing to make some sacrifices, even in personal desires, to achieve the end (e.g., by not eating certain foods one really likes or by staying at home instead of going to an event one really wants to attend).

Similarly, if the family is viewed as a community in the

191

biblical sense, then the aim of all its members (including the elderly) will be to promote the well-being of the whole, and whatever sacrifices are necessary to accomplish that end will not appear unreasonable or even contrary to one's *self*-interest. For instance, it may be, as pointed out earlier, that the adult child(ren)'s obligation to an older parent will not always be fulfilled best by coresidence; situations exist in which the best solution for all concerned is an alternative living arrangement, and all the parties should be willing to accept such a determination. As Daniel Callahan argues, however, "an inability to provide some kinds of care does not exempt children from providing other forms," including physical help (e.g., cleaning, shopping, transportation) and especially affection, the sharing of "that burden which few of us would care to bear alone—a recognition that life is gradually coming to an end and that nature is depriving us of our body, our individuality, and our future."[25] Whatever the specific practical solution devised, the Christian's obligations as presented in the sustaining story of the faith require the conclusion stated above: Adult children do have a responsibility for the welfare of their elderly parents.

A renewed sense of the family as community—a group of "intertwined lives" that share a common past and therefore are necessarily linked together in the present and for as long as their future exists—can be very beneficial to all those involved, both young and old. Such a concept is certainly more in line with the "sustaining story" that those who stand in the biblical tradition find in their foundational documents than is the attitude of narcissistic individualism that prevails today.

Conclusion

The current situation regarding aging and the elderly has been surveyed. Some of the major statements of the Bible—the foundational document of Christianity in which

the faithful discover the basis for their sustaining story—
have been examined. The questions of one's own aging and
of one's obligations toward the elderly have been considered
in the light of both the modern world and the sustaining
story. One final (and essential) point needs to be made, and
it must be stated without equivocation: Christian ethics
cannot be separated from Christian faith.

Christianity has many worthwhile things to say about how
human beings should feel about themselves and how they
should treat one another; certainly the world would be a
better place if everyone acted in accord with the teachings of
Jesus as presented in the Gospels. Indeed, both Judaism
and Christianity affirm that a vital religious faith—a sense of
God's presence in one's life ordering and directing one's
active response to God's gracious love—is the key to a
happy, satisfying life. This is as true in old age as at any other
stage of one's life, and it is also essential if one is to meet
one's obligation to the elderly.

At the heart of the Christian message, however—especially as presented by Paul—lies the claim that human
beings are *incapable* of acting as they ought, even if they
know what constitutes such action (see Rom. 7:15-20 for
the classic statement of this universal experience). To
simplify a complex situation, this incapacity is the result of
the original disobedience related in Genesis 3, in which
humanity's disordered relationships and fear of death are
both depicted as the consequence of alienation from God.
When one's relationship with God is disrupted, relationships with self, others, and even nature are also disordered.
As creatures in some fundamental way "like God" (i.e.,
created in God's own image), human beings can come to
know and to understand themselves fully only as they know
God more intimately. The possibility of gaining such
knowledge on one's own, however, is exactly what was lost
in the original disobedience.

From the Christian point of view, then, one can study Scripture and discover all that it has to say concerning attitudes about aging and obligations toward the elderly (indeed, one can know all there is to know from any perspective about all facets of gerontology), but all such knowledge is meaningless unless one *wants* to do something about it and *can* do something about it. After all, orthodox Christianity has never considered knowledge alone curative, a position that has led to the dismissal of all forms of Gnosticism as heretical. Rather, both Christianity and history combine to affirm that without a change of heart, human beings will not act upon any new knowledge in a meaningful or at least sustained way if such action is perceived to be contrary to their own self-interest. The Christian faith further claims that such a change requires repentance and rebirth, which in turn are possible only through the gracious intervention of God. ·

Thus when all the statistics have been cited, all the social critiques done, all the theological/ethical analyses presented, and all the specific suggestions made, biblical interpretations and rational arguments will ultimately have little impact as long as one's interest remains focused upon oneself. However trenchant the analyses of attitudes about aging and obligations toward the elderly, and however practical or idealistic the proposals for responding, without a reorientation of will even one's best intentions are sure to go awry.

The preeminent contribution that Christianity has to make to a study of aging and obligations toward the elderly, then, is *not* specific rules or even guidelines on the subject, helpful though they might be. Enough has been said about the difficulty of applying biblical texts directly to contemporary issues. Rather, Christianity offers precisely that which is most lacking in other approaches to coping with the inevitable deterioration and loss of vitality associated with growing older, as well as in other programs for meeting the very real needs of the elderly, namely, a means of overcoming the alienation from God and the consequent disordered relationships that are at the root of the human problem. In short, Christianity offers the means to the change of heart that is the only way to avoid treating the elderly (and, it should be noted, any other disadvantaged groups in society) as a "surplus population."

How then can one hope to accomplish what this study has suggested to be God's will for his human creatures with regard to aging and obligations toward the elderly? Christian theology responds that the only sure hope lies in hearing and believing the words that Paul once heard: "My grace is sufficient for you, for my power is made perfect in weakness" (2 Cor. 12:9). The *sine qua non* for receiving such grace and consequent power—as Paul's statement suggests and this book has argued—is a frank acknowledgment of one's weakness, insufficiency, and dependence upon the only true Source of grace, an acknowledgment that paradoxically may be greatly facilitated by the losses inherent in aging and may be demonstrated by caring for those who serve as vivid reminders of the ultimate finitude of all human beings.

NOTES

1. Christopher Lasch, *The Culture of Narcissism: American Life in an Age of Diminishing Expectations* (New York: W.W. Norton, 1978), pp. 10, 210.

2. Richard L. Rubenstein, *The Age of Triage: Fear and Hope in an Overcrowded World* (Boston: Beacon Press, 1983), p. 229.

3. For simplicity's sake, page references from this book will be in the text.

4. It should be noted that this mention of government policy is not meant to imply that the Bible (and the Christian ethics derived from it) can be applied simplistically to political issues. Neither, though, should the Christian's faith be a purely personal, private matter that has no relevance for her or his stance on social questions. Furthermore, as this book argues strongly, one who claims to follow

Jesus Christ is bound to act in certain ways toward those who are in need, especially in regard to one's own family.

5. Ernst Käsemann, *Commentary on Romans*, ed. and trans. Geoffrey W. Bromiley (Grand Rapids, Mich.: Wm. B. Eerdmans, 1980), p. 323.

6. Hans Walter Wolff, *Anthropology of the Old Testament*, trans. Margaret Kohl (Philadelphia: Fortress Press, 1974), p. 184.

7. Stanley Hauerwas and Richard Bondi, "Memory, Community and the Reasons for Living: Theological and Ethical Reflections on Suicide and Euthanasia," *Journal of the American Academy of Religion* 44 (1976): 439, 443. Crucial to the argument is their understanding of memory, which is not just "remembering" but "being present in mind," remaining always aware that the present is but a step on the way to the future; and "to have something 'present in mind' through memory is to have it here with us in all its creative force." Thus "memory has creative force when it reminds us not of past events but of the character which produced them, and when the memory of that character challenges us to renounce it or be true to it in the present moment" (p. 444). This concept contains rich possibilities for speaking to the problems inherent in applying the primary source of the Christian story (i.e., the Bible) to contemporary ethical issues.

8. Ibid., p. 445. This book can be seen as a response to another of their statements about the task of the theological ethicist: to seek "ways to form behavior and belief by the convictions which represent faithful expressions of the story that forms our Christian character."

9. Victoria Bumagin and Kathryn Hirn, *Aging Is a Family Affair* (New York: Thomas A. Crowell, 1979), p. 17.

10. Robert Butler, *Why Survive? Being Old in America* (New York: Harper & Row, 1975), p. 13. Michael Harrington (*The Other America: Poverty in the United States* [Baltimore: Penguin Books, 1962], p. 103) made a similar observation over two decades ago: "The image of a querulous, nagging, meandering old age is not a description of an ethical condition of human nature. It is, in part, the impression of what society has done to people by giving them meaningless years in which to live."

11. John LaFarge, S.J., *Reflections on Growing Old* (Garden City, N.Y.: Doubleday, 1963), p. 117.

12. Lisa Sowle Cahill, *Between the Sexes: Foundations for a Christian Ethics of Sexuality* (Philadelphia: Fortress Press; New York: Paulist Press, 1985), pp. 67, 73, 152. That the idea of community is regaining importance for discussions of issues such as care of the elderly is illustrated by the recent appearance of articles like Dan E. Beauchamp's "Community: The Neglected Tradition of Public Health," *Hastings Center Report* 15 (December 1985): 28-36.

13. Dianne Springer and Timothy Brubaker, *Family Caregivers and Dependent Elderly: Minimizing Stress and Maximizing Independence* (Beverly Hills: Sage Publications, 1984), p. 15.

14. Rolf Knierim, "Age and Aging in the Old Testament," in William M. Clements, ed., *Ministry with the Aging: Designs, Challenges, Foundations* (New York: Harper & Row, 1981), p. 29.

15. Quoted in Paul Ramsey, *Basic Christian Ethics* (New York: Charles Scribner's Sons, 1950), p. 95.

16. Daniel Callahan, "What Do Children Owe Elderly Parents?" *Hastings Center Report* 15 (April 1985): 36.

17. Gibson Winter, *Love and Conflict: New Patterns in Family Life* (Garden City, N.Y.: Doubleday, 1958), p. 181.

18. Any number of books—some quite good, others rather superficial and misguided—provide practical guidelines to apply when faced with a decision about the best type of care for an elderly member of the family. Some helpful ones are Victoria Bumagin and Kathryn Hirn, *Aging Is a Family Affair;* John Deedy, *Your Aging Parents* (Chicago: Thomas More Press, 1984); Dianne Springer and Timothy Brubaker, *Family Caregivers and Dependent Elderly;* and Barbara Silverstone and Helen Hyman, *You & Your Aging Parent,* updated and expanded ed. (New York: Pantheon Books, 1982).

19. Karl Barth, *The Humanity of God,* trans. John Newton Thomas and Thomas Wieser (Richmond: John Knox Press, 1960), p. 53.

20. Ramsey, *Basic Christian Ethics,* p. 93 (emphasis added).

21. Victor G. Cicirelli, "Adult Children and Their Elderly Parents," in Timothy H. Brubaker, ed., *Family Relationships in Later Life* (Beverly Hills: Sage Publications, 1983), p. 45. He observes that such a relationship "is characterized by closeness of feeling between parent and child, an easy compatibility between them, a low degree of conflict, and a good deal of satisfaction."

22. An interesting thought arises in this connection that echoes a concern of the last chapter. Historically, one of the reasons people care for the elderly has been the expectation that someone will do the same for them when they get old (conversely, one of the motivations for having children is to insure the parents' welfare in their old age). Today, however, people deny that they will get old and do everything they can to avoid showing that they are aging (a manifestation of the youth-oriented, death-denying attitude that values doing and having rather than being), thus implying that they will not need such care. One of the major traditional motivations for caring for the elderly therefore is removed, and if the younger members of society are to care for the older, the motivation must come from some other source, such as the one advocated in this book.

23. One organization that has recognized the importance of stronger marriages and healthier families in modern society is The Association for Couples in Marriage Enrichment (ACME), founded by David and Vera Mace, pioneers in marriage and family counseling. Information may be obtained by writing ACME, P.O. Box 10596, Winston-Salem, NC 27108.

24. Matilda White Riley, "The Family in an Aging Society: A Matrix of Latent Relationships," *Journal of Family Issues* 4 (September 1983): 446.

25. Callahan, "What Do Children Owe Elderly Parents?" p. 36.

BIBLIOGRAPHY

Books

Adamson, James. *The Epistle of James.* The New International Commentary on the New Testament. Grand Rapids, Mich.: Wm. B. Eerdmans Publishing Co., 1976.

The Babylonian Talmud. Seder Nashim. Vol. IV. Edited by Isidore Epstein; translated by H. Freedman. London: Soncino Press, 1936.

Bailey, Lloyd. *Biblical Perspectives on Death.* Biblical Theology Series, no. 5. Philadelphia: Fortress Press, 1979.

Barash, David P. *Aging: An Exploration.* Seattle: University of Washington Press, 1983.

Barth, Karl. *The Humanity of God.* Translated by John Newton Thomas and Thomas Wieser. Richmond: John Knox Press, 1960.

Binstock, Robert H., and Shanas, Ethel, eds. *Handbook of Aging and the Social Sciences.* 2d ed. New York: Van Nostrand Reinhold Co., 1985.

Birch, Bruce C., and Rasmussen, Larry L. *Bible and Ethics in the Christian Life.* Minneapolis: Augsburg Publishing House, 1976.

Blidstein, Gerald. *Honor Thy Father and Mother.* New York: KTAV Publishing House, 1975.

Bonhoeffer, Dietrich. *The Cost of Discipleship.* Rev. unabridged ed. Translated by R. H. Fuller. New York: Macmillan, 1959.

Brubaker, Timothy H. *Later Life Families.* Beverly Hills: Sage Publications, 1985.

————, ed. *Family Relationships in Later Life.* Beverly Hills: Sage Publications, 1983.

Bumagin, Victoria, and Hirn, Kathryn. *Aging Is a Family Affair.* New York: Thomas A. Crowell, 1979.

Butler, Robert. *Why Survive? Being Old in America.* New York: Harper & Row, 1975.

Buttrick, George A.; Bowie, Walter R.; Knox, John; Scherer, Paul; Terrien, Samuel; Harmon, Nolan P. *The Interpreter's Bible.* 12 vols. Nashville: Abingdon Press, 1952–57.

Buttrick, George A.; Kepler, Thomas S.; Knox, John; May, Herbert G.; Terrien, Samuel; and Bucke, Emory S., eds. *The Interpreter's Dictionary of the Bible.* 4 vols. Nashville: Abingdon Press, 1962.

Cahill, Lisa Sowle. *Between the Sexes: Foundations for a Christian Ethics of Sexuality.* Philadelphia: Fortress Press; New York: Paulist Press, 1985.

Cassuto, Umberto. *A Commentary on the Book of Exodus.* Translated by Israel Abrahams. Jerusalem: Magnes Press, 1967.

Childs, Brevard. *The Book of Exodus: A Critical, Theological Commentary.* Philadelphia: Westminster Press, 1974.

Chrysostom, Saint (John). *Saint Chrysostom: On the Priesthood; Ascetic Treatises; Select Homilies and Letters; Homilies on the Statues.* Vol. 9 of *A Select Library of the Post-Nicene Fathers of the Christian Church.* First series. Edited by Philip Schaff; translated by W. R. W. Stephens. Grand Rapids, Mich.: Wm. B. Eerdmans Publishing Co., n.d., reprinted 1978.

Clements, Ronald E. *Exodus.* The Cambridge Bible Commentary on the New English Bible. London: Cambridge University Press, 1972.

Clements, William M., ed. *Ministry with the Aging: Designs, Challenges, Foundations.* New York: Harper & Row, 1981.

Cohen, Stephen Z., and Gans, Bruce Michael. *The Other Generation Gap: The Middle-aged and Their Aging Parents.* Chicago: Follett Publishing Co., 1978.

Crim, Keith; Bailey, Lloyd R.; Furnish, Victor P.; and Bucke, Emory S. *The Interpreter's Dictionary of the Bible.* Supplementary volume. Nashville: Abingdon Press, 1976.

Crystal, Stephen. *America's Old Age Crisis.* New York: Basic Books, 1982.

Danby, Herbert. *The Mishnah.* Oxford: Oxford University Press, 1933.

Deedy, John. *Your Aging Parents.* Chicago: Thomas More Press, 1984.

Deeken, Alfons. *Growing Old, and How to Cope with It.* New York: Paulist Press, 1972.

Dibelius, Martin, and Conzelmann, Hans. *The Pastoral Epistles.* Hermeneia. Translated by Philip Buttolph and Adela Yarbro. Philadelphia: Fortress Press, 1972.

Fischer, David H. *Growing Old in America.* Expanded ed. New York: Oxford University Press, 1978.

Fromm, Erich. *To Have or To Be?* New York: Bantam Books, 1976.

Harrington, Michael. *The Other America: Poverty in the United States.* Baltimore: Penguin Books, 1962.

Herzog, Barbara Rieman, ed. *Aging and Income: Programs and Prospects for the Elderly.* The Gerontological Society, special publication no. 4. New York: Human Sciences Press, 1978.

Hessel, Dieter, ed. *Empowering Ministry in an Ageist Society.* New York: The Program Agency, United Presbyterian Church, U.S.A., 1981.

Käsemann, Ernst. *Commentary on Romans.* Edited and translated by Geoffrey W. Bromiley. Grand Rapids, Mich.: Wm. B. Eerdmans Publishing Co., 1980.

Köhler, Ludwig. *Old Testament Theology.* Translated by A. S. Todd. Philadelphia: Westminster Press, 1957.

Küng, Hans. *On Being a Christian.* Translated by Edward Quinn. Garden City, N.Y.: Doubleday & Co., 1976.

Kurtzman, Joel, and Gordon, Phillip. *No More Dying: The Conquest of Aging and the Extension of Human Life.* New York: Dell, 1977.

LaFarge, John, S.J. *Reflections on Growing Old.* Garden City, N.Y.: Doubleday & Co., 1963.

Lamm, Norman, ed. *The Good Society: Jewish Ethics in Action.* New York: Viking Press, 1974.

Lasch, Christopher. *The Culture of Narcissism: American Life in an Age of Diminishing Expectations.* New York: W. W. Norton and Co., 1978.

Lauterbach, Jacob Z., ed. and trans. *Mekilta de-Rabbi Ishmael.* 3 vols. Philadelphia: Jewish Publication Society of America, 1933.

LeFevre, Carol, and LeFevre, Perry, eds. *Aging and the Human Spirit: A Reader in Religion and Gerontology.* Chicago: Exploration Press, 1981.

Lohse, Eduard. *Colossians and Philemon.* Hermeneia. Translated by William R. Poehlmann and Robert J. Harris. Philadelphia: Fortress Press, 1971.

McKee, Patrick L., ed. *Philosophical Foundations of Gerontology.* New York: Human Sciences Press, 1982.

McKenzie, John L. *A Theology of the Old Testament.* Garden City, N.Y.: Doubleday Image Books, 1976.

Naisbitt, John. *Megatrends: Ten New Directions Transforming Our Lives.* Rev. ed. New York: Warner Books, 1984.

Nouwen, Henri J. M., and Gaffney, Walter J. *Aging: The Fulfillment of Life.* Garden City, N.Y.: Doubleday Image Books, 1974.

Ogletree, Thomas W. *The Use of the Bible in Christian Ethics: A Constructive Essay.* Philadelphia: Fortress Press, 1983.

Patai, Raphael. *Society, Culture, and Change in the Middle East.* 3d ed., enlarged. Philadelphia: University of Pennsylvania Press, 1969.

Pepper, Claude. *Ask Claude Pepper.* Garden City, N.Y.: Doubleday & Co., 1984.

Pritchard, James B., ed. *Ancient Near East Texts Relating to the Old Testament.* 3d. ed. Princeton: Princeton University Press, 1969.

Rad, Gerhard von. *Genesis: A Commentary.* Rev. ed. Translated by John H. Marks. Philadelphia: Westminster Press, 1972.

Ramsey, Paul. *Basic Christian Ethics.* New York: Charles Scribner's Sons, 1950.

Rhine, Shirley H. *America's Aging Population: Issues Facing Business and Society.* Report no. 785. New York: The Conference Board, 1980.

Robinson, H. Wheeler. *Corporate Personality in Ancient Israel.* Philadelphia: Fortress Press, 1964.

Robinson, J. A. T. *The Body: A Study in Pauline Theology.* London: S.C.M. Press, 1952.

Rosenfeld, Albert. *Prolongevity.* New York: Alfred A. Knopf, 1976.

Rubenstein, Richard L. *The Age of Triage: Fear and Hope in an Overcrowded World.* Boston: Beacon Press, 1983.

Sapp, Stephen. *Sexuality, the Bible, and Science.* Philadelphia: Fortress Press, 1977.

Silverstone, Barbara, and Hyman, Helen. *You & Your Aging Parent: The Modern Family's Guide to Emotional, Physical, and Financial Problems.* Updated, expanded ed. New York: Pantheon Books, 1982.

Simmons, Leo W. *The Role of the Aged in Primitive Society.* New Haven, Conn.: Yale University Press, 1945.

Smith, Harmon L. *Ethics and the New Medicine.* Nashville: Abingdon Press, 1970.

Springer, Dianne, and Brubaker, Timothy. *Family Caregivers and Dependent Elderly: Minimizing Stress and Maximizing Independence.* Beverly Hills: Sage Publications, 1984.

Stern, Aaron. *Me: The Narcissistic American.* New York: Ballantine Books, 1979.

Taylor, Vincent. *The Gospel According to St. Mark.* London: Macmillan & Co., 1959.

Toffler, Alvin. *The Third Wave.* New York: Bantam Books, 1980.

Turnage, Mac, and Turnage, Anne. *Graceful Aging: Biblical Perspectives.* Atlanta: Presbyterian Office on Aging, 1984.

Vriezen, Theodor. *An Outline of Old Testament Theology.* Translated by S. Neuijen. Newton, Mass.: Charles T. Branford Co., 1970.

Winter, Gibson. *Love and Conflict: New Patterns in Family Life.* Garden City, N.Y.: Doubleday & Co., 1958.

Wolff, Hans Walter. *Anthropology of the Old Testament.* Translated by Margaret Kohl. Philadelphia: Fortress Press, 1974.

Articles

Baldwin, Wendy H., and Nord, Christine W. "Delayed Childbearing in the U.S.: Facts and Fictions." *Population Bulletin* 39 (November 1984).

Beauchamp, Dan E. "Community: The Neglected Tradition of Public Health." *Hastings Center Report* 15 (December 1985): 28-36.

201

Borg, Marcus. "Death as the Teacher of Wisdom." *Christian Century* (February 26, 1986): 203-6.

Brody, Elaine. " 'Women in the Middle' and Family Help to Older People." *Gerontologist* 21 (1981): 471-80.

Callahan, Daniel. "What Do Children Owe Elderly Parents?" *Hastings Center Report* 15 (April 1985): 32-37.

Hauerwas, Stanley, and Bondi, Richard. "Memory, Community and the Reasons for Living: Theological and Ethical Reflections on Suicide and Euthanasia." *Journal of the American Academy of Religion* 44 (1976): 439-52.

Marty, Martin. *Context* (January 1, 1986): 4.

May, William F. "Who Cares for the Elderly?" *Hastings Center Report* 12 (December 1982): 31-37.

Ostling, Richard N. "Telling America What It Believes." *Time* (December 22, 1986): 59.

Palmore, Erdman. "Total Chance of Institutionalization Among the Aged." *Gerontologist* 16 (1976): 504-7.

Pratt, William F.; Mosher, William D.; Bachrach, Christine A.; and Horn, Marjorie C. "Understanding U.S. Fertility: Findings from the National Survey of Family Growth, Cycle III." *Population Bulletin* 39 (December 1984).

Program Resources Department, American Association of Retired Persons, and Administration on Aging, U.S. Department of Health and Human Services. "A Profile of Older Americans: 1986." Pamphlet. Washington, D.C., n.d. Based upon data compiled by Donald G. Fowles of the Administration on Aging.

Ramsey, Paul. "The Indignity of 'Death with Dignity.' " *Hastings Center Studies* 2 (May 1974): 47-62.

Riley, Matilda White. "The Family in an Aging Society: A Matrix of Latent Relationships." *Journal of Family Issues* 4 (September 1983): 439-54.

Santmire, Paul. "Nothing More Beautiful Than Death?" *Christian Century* (December 14, 1983): 1154-58.

Sapp, Stephen. ". . . As the Sparks Fly Upward." *Journal of Religion and Health* 16 (January 1977): 44-51.

Shanas, Ethel. "Social Myth as Hypothesis: The Case of the Family Relations of Old People." *Gerontologist* 19 (1979): 3-9.

———. "The Family as a Social Support System in Old Age." *Gerontologist* 19 (1979): 169-74.

———. "Older People and Their Families: The New Pioneers." *Journal of Marriage and the Family* 42 (February 1980): 9-15.

Smyer, Michael. "Aging and Social Policy: Contrasting Western Europe and the United States." *Journal of Family Issues* 5 (June 1984): 239-53.

INDEX

INDEX OF SCRIPTURE

Old Testament

Jeremiah	1:6 / 73
	1:7-8 / 95n
	7:5-7 / 76
	15:15-18 / 64
	26:17-19 / 74
Lamentations	5:12, 14 / 80
Ezekiel	20:21 / 91
	22:7 / 91
Daniel	3:1-7 / 61

Hosea	7:9 / 69
	11:2, 7 / 91
Amos	8:4, 10 / 76
Micah	6:8 / 122
	7:6 / 91, 131n, 168
Zechariah	8:4-5 / 70
	8:4, 8 / 81

New Testament

Matthew	5:3 / 115
	5:17-20 / 130n
	6:25-34 / 105
	6:27 / 105
	6:33 / 125
	7:17, 20 / 116-17
	10:21-22 / 131n
	10:34-39 / 125, 131n
	11:25 / 148
	13:44-45 / 125
	15:1-20 / 119
	15:17-20 / 186
	19:29 / 125
	22:34-40 / 111
	25:31-46 / 112, 116
	25:40 / 186
Mark	1:15 / 125
	1:20 / 117
	3:31-35 / 125
	3:33 / 126
	7:1-23 / 119, 180
	7:8-9, 11-12 / 119-20
	7:9-13 / 131n
	8:34-37 / 101

Mark, *cont.*	9:35 / 114
	10:17-22 / 178
	10:19 / 130n
	10:43-45 / 113
	12:28-34 / 122, 170-71
	13:12 / 131n
	14:36 / 101
Luke	1:7, 8, 18, 20, 36, 37 / 106
	2:25, 26, 29, 36-38 / 106-7
	16:20 / 115
	6:45 / 186
	7:22 / 115
	9:23-24 / 137
	9:59-62 / 125
	12:22-31 / 105
	14:12-14 / 114
	14:25-27 / 125
	14:26 / 126
	14:15-24 / 154
	18:1-8 / 142
	22:24-27 / 114
John	1:1, 14 / 100
	3:1-21 / 178
	3:4 / 111
	5:17-18 / 131n

INDEX OF SCRIPTURE